To ARChBishop.
Carlo Chaput.
May St. Pio of PIETRELCINA
inspire you and bless
you and your famiglia.
Graziella De Nunzio
Mandato

Grace Mandato
18 Longwood Ct. W
Harleysville, PA 19438

Padre Pio

*Encounters With A Spiritual
Daughter from Pietrelcina*

Padre Pio

*Encounters With A Spiritual
Daughter from Pietrelcina*

Graziella DeNunzio Mandato

Preface By the Most Reverend
James C. Timlin, D.D. Bishop of Scranton

A.M.  **D.G.**

A.M.  **D.G.**

Published by *A.M.D.G.*
Angelus Media Distribution Group
P.O. Box 3311
Sea Bright, New Jersey 07760
732.483.0800
http://shop.store.yahoo.com/amdg2000

ISBN:
ISBN: 0-9722044-0-7

Jacket Design by Brian Meulener

Printed and Bound in the United States of America

CONTENTS

PART ONE

Early Encounters with Padre Pio

PART TWO

San Giovanni Rotondo

PART THREE

Under Padre Pio's Guidance

PHOTOGRAPHS

From the Private Collection of Graziella DeNunzio Mandato

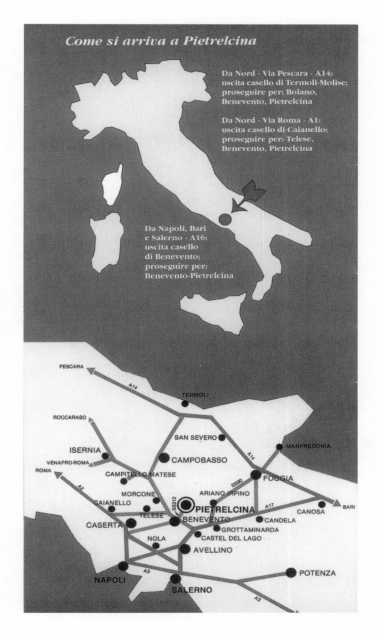

Courtesy: Comune di Pietrelcina

PREFACE

It is a pleasure to write a few words of introduction for the book by Graziella DeNunzio Mandato about Blessed Padre Pio.

Pope John Paul II, in his homily during the beatification of Blessed Padre Pio on May 2, 1999 said, "......by his life given wholly to prayer and to listening to his brothers and sisters, this humble Capuchin friar astonished the world. Those who went to San Giovanni Rotondo to attend his Mass, to seek his counsel or to confess to him, saw in him a living image of Jesus Christ suffering and risen. The face of Padre Pio reflected the light of the resurrection. His body, marked by the stigmata, showed forth the intimate bond between death and resurrection, which characterizes the paschal mystery."

The Holy Father stated that Padre Pio's face reflected the light of the resurrection. His very physical being, although scarred by suffering, radiated a life from the beyond, a human life that was transformed by God.

It was my great privilege to visit San Giovanni Rotondo in the winter of 1949 when I was a seminarian. I went to Padre Pio for confession, and along with the men in the sacristy, served his early morning Mass. It was a very moving moment, one I will never forget.

Men and women are drawn to the saints because they reflect in our earthly journey, the life of glory we all desire. May all those who read Graziella DeNunzio Mandato's personal encounters with Blessed Padre Pio increase in their desire for God and His Kingdom.

Bishop James C. Timlin

FORWARD

Dietrich Von Hildebrand once wrote that in the lives of the saints we see Christ. He shows Himself: "To see Me is to see the Father," (John 14:9) Jesus told Philip. In the saints, we not only see Christ, but we also touch Him and are touched by Him. My mother's beautiful experiences of her life, lived under Padre Pio's fatherly protection, point to and affirm this truth. Not only she, but multitudes have encountered the living Christ in the life of Saint Pio of Pietrelcina.

Growing up in an Italian household in which faith in the Lord was very real, concrete and never questioned – "Is He there or not?" – and where Christian life was as natural as the air one breathes, had a lot to do with the figure and personality of Padre Pio. I met him when I was a young boy, and along with my brother Vincent, was privileged to receive my First Holy Communion from him. More than my encounters with him, it was the influence of parents, grandparents, relatives and friends, all who knew him very well, which helped to form us into Christian followers of Christ.

My mother's recounting of her experiences with Padre Pio reads like the *Fioretti of St. Francis.* In Franciscan history, the *Fioretti* is a very popular account of the episodes in the life of St. Francis. It is not a strict historical study or the facts of St. Francis' life, rather, a "telling" of stories, experiences and anecdotes of the *Poverello's* life. Like the Gospel stories, it is more popular than an academic presentation. It is closer to life.

I think this type of story telling makes a story very attractive and enjoyable to read. Primarily, it contains the God-human encounter. God does love us, does guide us and does intervene in our daily lives, as Padre Pio's life so clearly shows.

In reading my mother's account, one is drawn into the fiber of her life, and it is easy to see the Lord acting in, and through, Padre Pio. In addition to encountering Christ through His servant Padre Pio, another truth is revealed to us: Our Lord not only wants to be seen, but He also wants to guide us. He wants to be our Shepherd.

Fyodor Dostoevsky, in his classic work *The Brothers Karamazov,* says that a spiritual father is "….a man who takes your soul and your will into his soul and his will." This is precisely what Padre Pio did with hundreds of thousands of people who met him in life. He led and bound them to Christ, if, of course, they were willing to be lead.

My mother's encounters with the Padre exemplify this relationship between a spiritual father and his daughter. My mother asked Padre Pio to be her spiritual father when she was still quite young – he agreed and never let her go. She often called him *"mio padruccio"* – my little father. The following pages display that, even to this day, he continues to guide and lead her in the Christian life, as well as prepare her for the Kingdom of the Father.

A final word about the last section of this book…..dreams. My mother recounts many dreams in which she believes that Padre Pio came to her to enlighten, assist or warn. I remember a wise philosophy professor, Fr. Joseph Occhio, S.D.B., who would tell us in class to "...ask the Lord to come to you and speak to you in your dreams. Yet, this doesn't mean that all "religious dreams" are a clear intervention of God's Spirit; discernment is always needed. Dreams can be an expression of one's inner life and desires and nothing more. They can also be of a diabolical nature or they can be of God.

My mother's life and devotion to Christ, and Padre Pio's presence in her life, demonstrates that the Lord can and does use any means to speak to us and lead us. The fruit of her dreams truly shows that Padre Pio spoke to her, and guided her during his lifetime and after his death. God, our Father, never abandons us and is forever inviting us into His eternal love.

Padre Pio's simple yet profoundly mysterious life – so immersed in the life of the living Christ – stands before us as a during his lifetime and after his death. God, our Father, never abandons us and is forever inviting us into His eternal love.

Padre Pio's simple yet profoundly mysterious life – so immersed in the life of the living Christ – stands before us as a powerful, shining light of God's presence among us. Those who encountered the Padre were immediately put in contact with God, His Kingdom and Eternity.

Graziella DeNunzio Mandato, who was given the privilege of being close to Padre Pio in her early life, wrote this simple text which allows the reader to enter into the mystery of the life of Christ, through His servant Padre Pio.

May Padre Pio, this wonderful human being so touched by God, bless you.

Fr. Pio Mandato, F.M.H.J.

THE TAU CROSS

This coat of arms has been the symbol of the Franciscans for many centuries. The image of the two crossed arms, each with a nail wound in the hand, represent both Christ and Saint Francis who received the Stigmata (the wounds of Christ) in his body two years before he died.

(2001 Capuchin Franciscan Friars of Australia)

INTRODUCTION

My name is Graziella DeNunzio Mandato and I live in Pennsylvania. My husband Andre, our three children and I immigrated to the United States of America in 1964 and settled in New Jersey.

I want to tell of all the encounters I have had with Padre Pio from the time I was a little girl living in Italy until my departure from my homeland.

I was born in Pietrelcina, Italy, in the province of Benevento. Pietrelcina is a small agricultural town with a population of about 3,000. In May of 1887, it became the birthplace of Francesco Forgione, who was to become beloved and renowned as Saint Pio of Pietrelcina, the first stigmatized, Capuchin priest.

My mother's name was Maria Pennisi and my father's Paris DeNunzio. Our house was located in the center of town on a street called Corso Padre Pio. The big parish church of Our Lady of the Angels could be seen from our home and this is where the beautiful statue of *La Madonna della Libera*, the protectress of Pietrelcina is still venerated. It was in this church that Padre Pio celebrated his first Mass on August 14, 1910, after his ordination in Benevento.

As I completed my testimony to Padre Pio, I was struck by the thought that never in my life have I ever considered writing a book. Maria Incremona, a good friend, once asked me, "Graziella, why don't you write your testimony about Padre Pio? You have had the great privilege of coming from his hometown. You knew him personally and have had the wonderful blessing of being his spiritual daughter." I responded by telling her, "It is impossible. I could never write such a book."

As the days passed, I began to reflect on the first time my father took me to meet Padre Pio in 1944. Then, I remembered the diaries I used to keep. I had recorded my confessional experiences with him as well as the counsel he gave me over the years. I had also written down the words he gave to me through my father when we came to the States. I had kept everything. Even the many stories my father had told me of the Padre were all written down and saved.

Padre Pio was always spoken of in our home. Friends of my father often visited, and each one would tell of their experiences with him and of the counseling they received when they visited him in San Giovanni Rotondo. In our town, Padre Pio was called *Il Monaco Santo*—the Holy Friar.

As a young girl I listened to everything that was being said about him. We all knew one another in town, and we all had great pride in being Padre Pio's *paesani,* that is, Padre Pio's townsfolk. My father worked in the city hall and during his free time he often went to visit his close friend, Padre Pio.

I gathered this material together and placed it on the dining room table to study. Slowly, I began to believe that a book might actually become a reality. In front of me rested the beautiful picture of Padre Pio, smiling. I stared at him and asked, "What must I do? Do I have to write this book? If you help me, I will try.

I would like to thank my son, Fr. Pio Mandato, for his time and patience in translating my "spiritual encounters" with Padre Pio and Bishop Timlin for his kindness in taking an interest in writing the Preface. My heartfelt thanks to Maria and Dick Incremona, who encouraged me to write the book and who brought the book to life. I would also like to thank Marion Gucker, Deidre McNamara, Nancy Savoca-Traub and Maralyn Campanella, all of whom gave graciously of their time and labor to bring this work to completion.

PART ONE

Early Encounters With Padre Pio

Testimony of My Father

When Padre Pio was still known as Francesco Forgione, the Padre and Zio (uncle) Mercurio Scocca became childhood friends. Both grew up in Piana Romana, on the outskirts of town. Mercurio's family had a little farm adjacent to that of Padre Pio's family. Mercurio and my father became close friends too. As an adult, Mercurio had a house next door to ours.

Mercurio spent a lot of time at our house and talked of his companionship with the Padre. They were so close that Padre Pio even baptized two of his sons. He described the Padre as being very affectionate, gentle, and prayerful, even as a child.

He also told us that one day Padre Pio's father, Orazio Forgione, wanted to dig a hole for a well in Piana Romana on their family farm. When the well was completed, no water was found. Francesco, who was a very young boy at the time, said, "Papa, why don't you dig another hole in this place?" Orazio responded in a serious but joking manner, "Francesco, if there is no water there, I'll throw you into the hole." After Orazio dug the hole, water flowed and Francesco remained safe!

One morning in the summer of 1943, my father turned to my mother and said, "I am going to San Giovanni Rotondo to visit Padre Pio." Whenever he went to visit the Padre, he would always bring broccoli from his

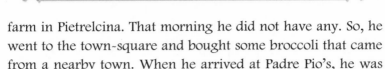

farm in Pietrelcina. That morning he did not have any. So, he went to the town-square and bought some broccoli that came from a nearby town. When he arrived at Padre Pio's, he was very happy to see him and said, "Father, I brought you broccoli from Pietrelcina." Padre Pio looked at him and said with a smile, "Paris, thank you for your good intention, but this broccoli is not from Pietrelcina." My father was amazed and did not know what to say. The Padre embraced him and took him upstairs to his room, where he asked many questions about his beloved Pietrelcina and the townspeople.

Later in Padre Pio's cell, the Padre noticed that my father, who stood close to his nightstand, took some handkerchiefs and a glove that Padre Pio used to cover his wounds. The Padre asked, "Paris, what are you doing? Are you a thief too?" My father put those mementos into his pocket as Padre Pio smiled and said nothing else. When he returned home, my father placed the handkerchiefs in a drawer. But the glove was left on the dresser to be venerated.

Whenever I met people who were devoted to Padre Pio, I would cut off little pieces from the glove and give them out, especially to the sick. When my father found out what I was doing, I had to run and hide from him.

A story my father once told me took place in the early 60's. My father and some friends were driving to San Giovanni Rotondo from Pietrelcina, a drive of two and a half hours. The exhausted driver struggled to stay awake, however, he eventually fell asleep at the wheel.

My father was frightened. He invoked Padre Pio and prayed, "Help us!" The road that climbed up the Gargano to San Giovanni Rotondo was steep, winding and dangerous. The car veered off the road, but the driver woke up at the last second, in time to control the car. My father kept on repeating, "Padre, help us!"

When they arrived at the friary, they went upstairs to see Padre Pio in his cell. My father said, "Padre, at last we are here. We were frightened." Padre Pio asked, "Paris, you were afraid?" "Yes, Padre," he replied. Padre Pio questioned, "Who do you think was driving the car? Didn't you know it was I?" "Thank you, Padre Pio!" they all replied.

Again in the 60's, my father went to Padre Pio with Mercurio and another friend. When they arrived in San Giovanni Rotondo, they rented a room for the night. My father slipped on the floor and injured himself. In fact, he could not move and had to rest in bed. Zio Mercurio and the other friend went on ahead to see Padre Pio. Before they had a chance to inform the Padre of my father's fall, he asked, "And where is Paris?" "He couldn't come," they replied, "he fell." Padre Pio said, "How it disappoints me. He is a holy man." The following day my father had recovered sufficiently to visit Padre Pio. As soon as the Padre saw my father, he warmly embraced him and my father quickly felt better. My father then thanked the Padre for his help and kissed his hand.

Another time when my father was visiting Padre Pio, he found the Padre surrounded by many friars, doctors and friends. Everyone was speaking. My father watched Padre Pio and thought to himself how he would love to kiss his hand, but the Padre was in such demand that my father could not get close enough. Meanwhile, Padre Pio looked over at him and said, "Paris, there no need to think about it. Come and kiss my hand." My father was elated. Padre Pio not only let him kiss his hand, he also read his thoughts.

A priest's hand is normally venerated because it is the instrument that changes the bread and wine into the Body and Blood of Christ. In Padre Pio's case, his hands also bore the wounds of Christ. It was for this reason only, and not for personal aggrandizement, that he allowed his hands to be kissed.

My First Meeting With Padre Pio

All of these beautiful accounts of Padre Pio fascinated me and a desire grew within me to meet him. Until this time I had only seen him in photographs, but when I was ten years old my father told me, "I will take you to San Giovanni Rotondo."

We traveled by train from Benevento to Foggia and from Foggia took a bus, which brought us to San Giovanni Rotondo an hour later. In all, the journey took three hours.

Arriving in San Giovanni Rotondo, we went to the friary church, the small original Church of Our Lady of Grace. On the right side of the main altar I saw a door surrounded by a group of women. I was in the back of the group and being small, could only see Padre Pio's head. While everyone was kissing his hand, I looked up and noticed Padre Pio staring at me. He extended his arm over some of the ladies and allowed me to kiss his hand as well. His eyes made an intense impression on me and for the first time, I smelled the scent of perfume that would always be associated with him.

When we returned home to Pietrelcina, I continuously thought about Padre Pio and had a great desire to visit him again. I would return innumerable times, just to be close to him and sometimes these trips would last for several months.

Padre Pio and Pietrelcina

When I was in elementary school in Pietrelcina, my teacher was Graziella Pannullo, the niece of Father Salvatore Pannullo, Pietrelcina's parish priest. During class, she would speak to us about Padre Pio. In school, she led us in the daily rosary, and we prayed for Padre Pio and for his mission at San Giovanni Rotondo.

After completing school, I went to the religious sisters to be taught embroidery. We spoke of Padre Pio there as well and often went with the choir to sing in the main church, where Padre Pio had been known to pray for many hours. Many of the stories Miss Pannullo repeated were from her uncle. Padre Pio lived in Pietrelcina from 1909 to 1916 and he was very close to Father Salvatore.

When Padre Pio was a young boy tending the family sheep as they grazed in the pastures of Piana Romana, his neighbors often saw him on his knees with a rosary in his hands. He was also known to make small crosses out of wood at that time. People who knew him then often remarked that young Francesco was a little saint.

Father Salvatore loved Francesco like a son and when Francesco came home from the seminary, where he was studying for the priesthood, they often visited with each other. The young Padre was known to pray for hours in the church and Father Salvatore would customarily leave him there. Returning much later, he would often find the Padre in ecstasy.*

One day after Mass, Michele Pilla, the sacristan, had to lock and secure the church. Often Michele would lock Padre Pio in, since he would spend hours in prayer and thanksgiving after offering Mass. On one occasion, Michele found the young priest seemingly unconscious. Frightened, he ran to Father Salvatore who told him not to disturb the Padre. "Do your cleaning," he advised, "and ring the bell at noon."

Another time, Michele found Padre Pio in the church and this time he appeared to have died. Again, Michele went to Father Salvatore who said, "Don't be alarmed, all will be well. Padre Pio is in ecstasy." During these times of prayer, Padre Pio was unaware of anything happening around him.

Frequently, Father Salvatore and the young Padre would go for long, prayerful walks together. On one such walk, Francesco stopped suddenly and said, "I hear a choir of angels and bells in this place. Do you hear them?" Father Salvatore answered, "No." Francesco then said, "Here in this place will one day be a Capuchin friary."

The friary was eventually built and dedicated in 1945. Mary Pyle, an American spiritual daughter of Padre Pio, who settled in San Giovanni Rotondo donated the funds for the construction.

*Ecstasy (Ecstatic Union) is the state of being beside oneself through some overpowering experience. Many saints have received ecstasies as a supernatural gift from God, although ecstasy of itself is not a criterion of holiness.

After Padre Pio was ordained a priest on August 10th in 1910, he remained in Pietrelcina for seven years because of poor health. One of the most incredible stories Miss Pannullo shared with my classmates and me was about the wounds suffered by the young Padre in 1910. Padre Pio frequently went to Piana Romana. Here he would spend his days in the open air with Jesus and the angels. His favorite place of prayer was sitting on a big rock under a certain elm tree. He referred to this rock as *la mia poltrona*, which means, my armchair, for it was here that he liked to sit.

It was during one of these dialogues with Jesus that he felt a puncture in the middle of each hand. Padre Pio went to Father Salvatore and told him about his wounds and Father Salvatore advised him to get them examined by Dr. Andrea Cardone.

The doctor didn't know how to explain this phenomenon. However, when he pressed his fingers into the center of Padre Pio's hands, it caused the Padre great pain. Padre Pio joked with the doctor and asked, "Are you trying to be like St. Thomas?"

Padre Pio was embarrassed to be noticed by the townspeople. He prayed to Jesus that the wounds would become invisible. Though they remained invisible for eight years, the pain from these wounds continued to cause him a great deal of suffering.

Later, a chapel dedicated to Saint Francis of Assisi was built in Piana Romana along side the elm tree where

Padre Pio received his wounds in 1910. Today the trunk of this same elm tree is preserved, enclosed and protected from devoted relic seekers.

Lucia Iadanza, a spiritual daughter of the Padre, once told my young classmates and me that on December 24, 1922, she went to San Giovanni Rotondo for Christmas, simply to be near Padre Pio. He was her confessor and she was very devoted to him.

Since it was Christmas, the friars brought a brazier into the sacristy. There were three women waiting for Padre Pio's midnight Mass to begin. The women eventually fell asleep, but Lucia remained awake and continued praying the rosary. Suddenly, Padre Pio came into the sacristy from the friary stairs. He stopped when a ray of illuminating light appeared. Inside the light was the Infant Jesus, who eventually settled Himself into the arms of the Padre. Padre Pio's face reddened, then radiated. When the Infant Jesus disappeared, Padre Pio realized that Lucia was watching him with awe. He came close to her and said, *"Lucia, che hai visto?"* (What did you see?) She replied, "Padre, I saw everything." Padre Pio became very stern and said, "Do not say anything to anyone about what you saw." It was many years later that she finally told this story.

Mary Pyle

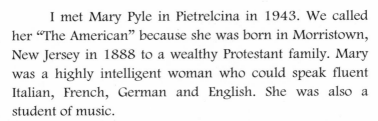

I met Mary Pyle in Pietrelcina in 1943. We called her "The American" because she was born in Morristown, New Jersey in 1888 to a wealthy Protestant family. Mary was a highly intelligent woman who could speak fluent Italian, French, German and English. She was also a student of music.

Mary came to Italy and met Dr. Maria Montessori, who resided in Rome and was a devout Catholic. Eventually, Mary converted to the Catholic faith. Hearing about Padre Pio, she went to San Giovanni Rotondo in 1923 with the decision to live near him. She built a large house for herself, not far from the friary, and became a Third Order Franciscan. She wore the brown habit and white cord of St. Francis.

During World War II she was advised to go to Pietrelcina. She lived there from 1941 to 1943 in the house where Padre Pio was raised. It was during this time that my mother had a dream about Padre Pio in which he asked her, "Why don't you go and visit Mary Pyle, the American sister?" My mother responded, "I am too shy." Padre Pio said, "You go and tell her that I sent you."

She decided to go and took me along as well. When my mother told Mary of her dream about Padre Pio, Mary became overwhelmed with happiness and began to cry. She had my mother recount the dream two more times.

She then asked me my name, embraced me and said, "Whenever you come to San Giovanni Rotondo, come visit me." I was still only ten years old at the time.

Often, when I went to see Padre Pio after his Mass, Mary would lean on my arm as I accompanied her home; then I would stay for dinner at her house. Since she was very hospitable, her home was always filled with frequent guests. It was in this home that I saw the room where Padre Pio's mother, Giuseppa DeNunzio, usually stayed and where she eventually died in 1929.

Recollections of Padre Pio's Family

I remember the friendship that existed between my family and that of Zio Michele, Padre Pio's brother. Zio Michele often came to our house. He was a man who always wore a smile, and we had great affection for each other. He loved playing cards with my father while my mother served him coffee. He told us numerous stories about his brother.

One story took place when Francesco Forgione was ten years old. His father took him to a nearby sanctuary where the Feast of San Pellegrino was being celebrated. When they entered the church, Francesco noticed a mother crying and praying out loud to God. It seemed that her child was very ill and Francesco began to pray for the child. It was understood by all that the child recovered!

I remember another story Zio Michele told that took place when Francesco was 12 years old. Young Francesco developed an intestinal disturbance and became ill. The doctor was called and gave him medication, but the doctor was not hopeful that the boy would recover. Francesco asked his mother to take him to Piana Romana where they had their little farm which produced crops of grain. Once there, Giuseppa Forgione prepared a large dish of spicy fried peppers for the farm workers. Young Francesco went to bed while everyone else remained out in the fields.

Eventually he got up and saw the fried peppers. He ate a fair amount of them and went back to bed. He then began to sweat profusely. When Michele came in and saw his brother's condition, he became very concerned. Francesco asked him for water to quench his thirst. Some time later, when his mother came in and noticed the missing peppers, Francesco admitted that he had eaten them. After this, his intestinal problem completely disappeared.

There were other members of Padre Pio's family with whom we were friendly. Pia Forgione, Zio Michele's daughter, was my godmother for confirmation. My mother had asked Pia Forgione if she would be my Godmother and she readily accepted. I was confirmed by the Bishop of Benevento and was very happy that my godmother was one of Padre Pio's relatives.

Ettore Masone, the son of Padre Pio's sister, Felicita, was another family friend. He would come to visit and spend a good deal of time with our family.

Healings

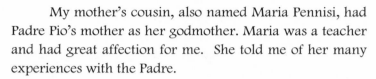

My mother's cousin, also named Maria Pennisi, had Padre Pio's mother as her godmother. Maria was a teacher and had great affection for me. She told me of her many experiences with the Padre.

One story she told my mother was of her diagnosis of tuberculosis in 1926. She was under the care of a famous doctor, Giuseppe Moscati from the University of Napoli, who was beatified by Pope Paul VI in 1975. Maria's situation was hopeless. She battled high fevers and hemorrhaged a great deal. Maria's father, Uncle Carmine and her mother took her to San Giovanni Rotondo to see Padre Pio. As soon as he saw her, he placed his hands on her shoulders and silently prayed. When they returned to Pietrelcina, Maria found she was completely cured. She lived until 1990, sixty four years after she was originally diagnosed.

Another story of Padre Pio's abilities, one which was a popular discussion among his friends, centered on a young girl named Gemma Di Giorgio. In 1933 she was born blind, having no pupils in her eyes. On the advice of a religious sister, her grandmother took her to see Padre Pio. She was seven years of age at the time, and, during this visit, Gemma went to Padre Pio for confession. He blessed her and made the sign of the cross over her eyes. Gemma received an unbelievable grace; she was able to see normally despite the fact that she had no pupils. I marveled when I heard this story.

The story of yet another healing, performed by Padre Pio in 1950, was told to my mother by Anita Nardella. Anita's son, who lived in Northern Italy, had friends whose son was mute from birth. He was only eight years old and the many doctors who saw him offered the parents no hope. The boy's mother wanted to take her son to San Giovanni Rotondo to see Padre Pio, but her husband refused. After much persistence, the father, who was a non-believer, finally gave in. However, he made the condi-tion that he would not enter the church when his wife and son were to meet with the Padre. When they arrived at the Capuchin friary, the mother and son entered the church while he waited outside in the piazza underneath a tree. Padre Pio was hearing confessions and after some time, he motioned to the boy to come over to him. The boy approached Padre Pio and heard him say, "Go outside and call your father." The boy immediately went outside and spoke for the first time saying, "Papa, Padre Pio told me to tell you that you have to go inside."

Sometimes, Padre Pio was the recipient of blessings as well. The famous Italian tenor, Beniamino Gigli, visited with Padre Pio one day. As they walked in the garden at the friary, the great tenor asked the Padre if he would like to hear a song. He replied, "Yes, sing the song *Mamma*." The Padre listened and was deeply pleased.

My Second Visit With Padre Pio

I was 15 years old the second time I went to San Giovanni Rotondo, again accompanied by my father. When we first arrived, we went to a small hotel to reserve a room for the night, since we planned on leaving the next day.

As soon as I entered the room, I felt ill and had to rest in bed. My father said, "Graziella, you rest and I'll go visit Padre Pio." It was still afternoon, and I did not tell my father the nature of my discomfort.

My father went to the friary garden and found Padre Pio surrounded by many people. Padre Pio spotted my father and he called to him saying, "Paris, where is your daughter Graziella?" He replied, "Padre, she had to go to bed because she was not feeling well." Padre Pio said, "Don't worry, for she has the same concern that all women have." My father became embarrassed

When he returned to the hotel, he asked me, "Why didn't you tell me the reason you weren't feeling well?" I answered, "I felt that I could not discuss such personal matters." Padre Pio, however, knew all things.

The next day Padre Pio heard my confession. I knelt in front of him while he was in the confessional. He extended his hand for me to kiss and gave me rosary beads, as well as a small medal. The rosary had large beads, which were a beautiful gray color, and they emitted a fragrant aroma.

Later, my father went upstairs to Padre Pio's cell to speak with him. There was a distant family relationship between my grandfather Antonio DeNunzio and Padre Pio's mother, Giuseppa DeNunzio. Padre Pio, as always, asked him many things about Pietrelcina. He loved my father, and there was a wonderful closeness between them, despite the fact that my father was nine years younger than the Padre.

When we returned home, I immediately showed everyone the rosary beads Padre Pio had given me, and all were surprised at the sweet scent of roses emanating from them. Every evening we recited the rosary in our home and our neighbor's frequently joined us. My mother was very devoted to *La Madonna della Libera*. Sometimes, our Lady came to her in dreams.

Once Padre Pio came to my mother in a dream and asked, "Maria, after the rosary, why don't you recite the *Hail Holy Queen?*" My mother responded, "I don't remember it." Padre Pio then said, "Well, I'll recite it, and you say it after me." When she awoke in the morning, she knew the prayer by heart.

For two years I cherished the rosary beads Padre Pio had given me. Then I gave them away as a gift to Antonio Sagliocca. He was a friend of the family and a benefactor from New York. It was Antonio who would have a convent built for the sisters in Pietrelcina.

During a visit to my parents' home, he stayed to pray the rosary with us. He became moved at the sight of my rosary beads and asked if I would give them to him. I agreed because he was so generous with the sisters. Antonio then said, "I'm grateful to you, but I wouldn't have given them away for a million dollars."

Everyone told me I should have kept them, but, because of my act of gratitude toward Antonio, Padre Pio eventually gave me another pair. Antonio Sagliocca has since died, and at times I wonder where those beautiful beads are and if they still give off a pleasing fragrance?

My Third Visit to San Giovanni Rotondo

As we were preparing to leave for my third visit with the Padre, my father and I happened to be walking by the home of Dr. Andrea Cardone. He was a good friend of both my father and the Padre. Since he was the town doctor and Pietrelcina was like a large family, he was friendly with everyone.

We were about to catch a bus to go to Benevento and then on to San Giovanni Rotondo, when Dr. Cardone saw us. He said to me, "Graziella, as soon as you see Padre Pio, tell him that I send my greetings."

When we arrived in San Giovanni Rotondo, I went to Padre Pio for confession. Confession with the Padre was always a moving experience. Padre Pio didn't give you a chance to speak because he was the one who said everything; he told you your sins. I always responded by saying, "Yes, Padre." Then he would give me absolution.

After confession, I knelt as usual, facing him, for his blessing. He said, "So you didn't tell me that you saw Dr. Cardone this morning in Pietrelcina and that he sends me his greetings!" "Oh, Padre, please excuse me. Yes, he sends his greetings," I said. Padre Pio smiled and extended his hand for me to kiss. Seeing that I was upset with myself, he gave me a small religious medal with Our Lady's image on one side and St. Michael's on the other.

Dr. Cardone was the same doctor who at the insistence of Father Salvatore Pannullo, examined Padre Pio after he received the invisible stigmata while in Piana Romana. The Padre had great respect for Dr. Cardone, who would often visit with the Padre at San Giovanni Rotondo. Dr. Cardone was born in 1876 and died in 1969, the year following Padre Pio's death

Padre Pio and Bilocation*

In moments of important decisions, my family always sought the counsel of Padre Pio. One would usually seek advice from him during confession, but Padre Pio was close to us in many other ways. An example of his "closeness" occurred in our home in 1945.

Our home was a stone house with four large rooms upstairs. One evening, while I was downstairs in the dining room embroidering, my parents had just gone upstairs to retire and say their prayers. Suddenly, they heard three knocks on the roof. These three knocks brought my parents a sense of joy. At first, they didn't tell me anything about this, to protect me from becoming frightened.

On another evening when I decided to retire early, As I reached the top of the stairs, I heard three loud knocks. I went to look outside on the balcony and saw nothing. I then went into my parents' room and saw that they were in good humor. I told them what I had heard, but they said, "Graziella, don't be afraid; it is nothing."

Shortly afterward, my father went to visit Padre Pio. He said, "Padre, when we retire at night, we hear a loud knocking on the roof, and it brings us joy. Is it you coming to greet us?" Padre Pio laughed and didn't respond, but my father understood it to mean that it was indeed the Padre.

This confirmed our original belief that it was Padre Pio, greeting us, through the gift of Bilocation, during one of his mysterious trips to various places around the world.

Bilocation is the actual presence of one finite person in two places at the same time. Explanation taken from The Catholic Encyclopedia, Thomas Nelson Publishers, 1976, p 75.

PART TWO

San Giovanni Rotondo

Living in San Giovanni Rotondo

My mother's dear friend, Angelina DeStefano from Pietrelcina, came to visit. She told us that she had just built a house in San Giovanni Rotondo. It was near the friary and close to Mary Pyle's home. Angelina wanted to live near Padre Pio. She invited my mother to visit her and my mother asked if I could go alone and spend some time there. Angelina said that she wanted to ask Padre Pio about it first.

One day while the Padre was hearing her confession, she told him that Graziella, daughter of Maria and Paris DeNunzio, wanted to spend some time with her. She asked him for his opinion. He replied, "Indeed, have her come. She will be good company for you."

I was overjoyed at the thought of being near Padre Pio and having him hear my confession frequently. It was during my second visit to the Padre, when I was fifteen, that my desire to be near him increased. My first stay with Angelina was for two weeks. During another visit, I remained for a month.

It was at the end of one visit, right after confession, that I knelt in front of Padre Pio and asked, "Padre, will you accept me as your spiritual daughter?" He placed his hand on my head and said, "Of course, I accept you as my spiritual daughter! Behave well." Then he blessed me. I was very moved and kissed his hand.

Afterwards, I went to Angelina and told her. She said, "Very good. How blessed you are. Padre Pio has taken you under his protection. From now on you must obey all that he tells you." This I did willingly. That evening Angelina led me in reciting the fifteen decades of the rosary.

Every morning we rose at 4 a.m. to go to the front of the chapel of St. Francis and wait for the doors to open for the Padre's 5 a.m. Mass. This took place in the friary church. We literally ran to get close enough to the altar whenever he celebrated Mass. Then everyone knelt and remained in silence for an hour and a half.

Angelina often said, "Padre Pio knows all." Sometimes when she and her friends gossiped a little too harshly, she heard about it from the Padre during her next confession. He would say, "Will you stop criticizing others! You should want to be good and pray." Angelina told me, "We must be good, even in our speech. If not, he will reprimand us."

Many people went to visit Padre Pio, and after attending his Mass, the crowds would gather in the piazza outside the church and sit beneath a big tree. During these moments, everyone took turns describing personal encounters with the Padre.

Once a woman began crying, and I asked her why. She said sadly, "Padre Pio didn't give me absolution because I had an abortion." Normally, a priest does not refuse absolution for regretted sins. However, Padre Pio with his gift of reading souls, would know when a penitent did not recognize the gravity of his or her offense. He always prayed, and suffered greatly for such penitents and most, of course, re-ordered their lives as a result of his intervention.

At times, Padre Pio would refuse absolution to lead people to true repentance and to make them realize the gravity of their sins. These people were either drawn back to him for another confession or went to another priest for absolution.

There were two lines leading to his confessional. One line was for foreigners or people from out-of-town. The other line was for the townspeople. It was on the latter line that I waited for confession every week. I noticed how my joy increased and I felt that way all day because I was able to be around the Padre. When he listened to the women's confessions, the confessional remained open. We could see him and he could watch us at the same time.

Directly after Mass, Padre Pio heard the men's confessions. Later, from 9 a.m. until 11a.m., he heard the women's confessions. After my confession was heard, I remained in church to pray the rosary and attend other Masses.

Padre Pio once said to me, "You were just here two days ago." "Padre," I said, "I came to kiss your hand." He let me kiss his hand and said, "These Pietrelcinese!" By saying this, he conveyed to me that people from Pietrelcina were highly regarded by him.

On another occasion, Padre Pio reached into his pocket and gave me some candies that had been given to him. I still have them preserved as a memento. I have also saved the medals of Our Lady and St. Michael that he gave me on other occasions.

One morning, prior to Mass, I was able to get close enough to the altar to kneel at the altar rail. Everyone was kneeling silently in prayer. As the Padre approached the altar, his face became reddened, then illuminated. Tears started to fall as he began Mass because he was gazing on the living Christ.

Everyone was able to see the mystical suffering in Padre Pio. The Holy Spirit was upon him and his face took on changes even as we watched him. At the beginning of Mass his face was red. During the celebration, he was transformed and his face took on the features of suffering and became pallid. He prayed for those who asked him for help and for those who were far from home. He also prayed for the sick and the diseased.

Sometimes he would rest his elbows on the altar, motionless. His Mass lasted about an hour and a half. Everyone watched him with intense emotion and only those who have had the privilege of attending his Masses can truly understand what it was like. By the time Mass was over, he was totally absorbed in it. One could see the stigmata on his hands because he did not wear gloves during the Mass.

On another occasion as he descended the altar,

I arose and drew close to him and was able to kiss his hand directly on the wound. He looked and said nothing. I was filled with happiness and for the rest of the day, I smelled the scent of roses.

After Mass, we would wait in church until he heard confession, then, he would give us Holy Communion. Before Vatican II in Italy, Holy Communion was distributed after Mass. In the evening, we went to church for the Benediction of the Blessed Sacrament, officiated by Padre Pio. After supper, again, we went to the friary where Padre Pio peered out of the window in his cell and waved to us with his handkerchief. We all shouted, *"Buona notte, Padre!"* (Good night, Father)

I developed many friendships in San Giovanni Rotondo. One was with Gaitanina, the niece of Brother Gerardo who was the porter, or church doorkeeper. He often let us enter by the side of the church. Once, when Padre Pio walked past us I said, "Padre, I call you *Padruccio."* *Padruccio* is a term of affection that means "Little Father." He responded kindly, "One doesn't need to be a fortune teller to know that." He loved to joke, and it was his way of telling me that he already knew. From then on I openly called him *Padruccio.*

When I became 18 on November 1st, after making my confession to the Padre, I knelt before him saying, "Padre, today is the Feast of the Immaculate Conception. Will you consecrate me to the Madonna?" Padre looked gently down on me and with both hands touched my hand

and said, "Yes, I will consecrate you to her."

I was elated when he consecrated me to the Mother of Jesus and from that day on I have always felt her presence within me. I have such great devotion to her, that when I see images of her I am moved to tears and just thinking about her brings me pleasure. Padre Pio used to say, "Love the Madonna, and bring others to love her."

From the day that Padre Pio consecrated me to the mother of Jesus, I have recited the rosary daily. In the beginning, I prayed it at home with my parents and later in life, I prayed it with my husband and three sons.

The Gift of Another Rosary

One evening, while having supper with Angelina de Stefano at her house in San Giovanni Rotondo, I heard a voice shouting my name from outside. "Graziella! Graziella!" I went outside and saw Petruccio Cugino, who was blind. I used to see him at the side of the altar when Padre Pio celebrated Mass and I knew him well.

"Petruccio, what is the matter?" I asked. "I have a gift for you. The Padre has sent you a rosary," he replied. I happily took the rosary and thanked him. I told Angelina and then thought about the other rosary I had given Antonio Sagliocca. I still have this second rosary and every day I pray on it to our Heavenly Mother.

The Padre would frequently say, "Our Lady wishes to be served by praying the Blessed Rosary in order to give us graces and blessings."

My Mother Confesses to Padre Pio

In 1942 my mother went to confession to Padre Pio. He told her, "Maria, you have to have another child." "Padre," she said, "I have already had seven and now I am 38 years old." When she admitted to no longer having full union with my father, he corrected her and advised her that they both needed to fulfill their marital obligations.

In 1943, my mother gave birth to a boy whom they named Pio Francesco. Padre Pio was delighted, especially when parents named their children after him.

A Dear Friend - Cosimo Iadanza

Cosimo Iadanza, and another good family friend from Pietrelcina, was told by the Padre that his wife Grazia was pregnant. Padre Pio asked, "Cosimo, do you like my name?" "Yes, Padre," Cosimo replied. "Then give him my name," said the Padre, since he already knew it was to be a boy. He was born the same year as my brother Pio.

A number of years later, Cosimo brought his son Pio to meet the Padre. After being introduced, Padre Pio said, "This boy will one day be mayor of Pietrelcina." This prophecy was fulfilled and Pio held the office of mayor of Pietrelcina from 1986 to 1997.

A number of years after the birth of little Pio, Cosimo's wife became pregnant with another child. Cosimo went to Padre Pio and asked for his blessing on her new pregnancy. Padre Pio told him, "All will go well. You will have two little girls, and they will both become religious sisters." This prophecy was fulfilled as well, and indeed, they both became religious sisters. I see them every year when I return to Pietrelcina, and both are filled with goodness.

My Brother's Confirmation

My father became friendly with Count Giovanni Telfener, a noble person, who for the love of Padre Pio, settled in San Giovanni Rotondo with his wife. When my older brother Antonio asked the Count if he would be his godfather for confirmation, he said he wanted to ask Padre Pio before responding.

The Count found the Padre, who was surrounded by friars and friends, and stated, "Padre, there is young man, Antonio DeNunzio from Pietrelcina, who has asked that I be his godfather." Padre Pio said, "Of course you must be his godfather. Antonio is a relative."

I remember the Count coming to Pietrelcina, staying at our house and going to the cathedral in Benevento for my brother's Confirmation. Whenever we visited him in San Giovanni Rotondo, we always found him to be of a kind nature.

Family Experiences

I wanted to spend Christmas of 1946 in San Giovanni Rotondo. Beautiful stories had been told to me of Padre Pio's celebrations at Christmas, especially when he carried the Baby Jesus in procession.

San Giovanni Rotondo is known to be cold and windy in the winter because it is located in the mountains. When I mentioned the weather to Padre Pio, I simply stated, "Padre, it is very cold." He laughed and responded, "If you are cold, light a fire and you will warm up."

My brother Antonio came a few days before Christmas that year to bring me home and we went together to see the Padre. I told Padre Pio my brother wanted to take me back with him to Pietrelcina, but I preferred to stay here in San Giovanni Rotondo.

The Padre smiled and said, "You tell him." "Padre," I asked, "May I kiss the wound on your foot?" He said, "What do you think, that I am going to take off my socks and sandals so you can kiss my foot!" He placed his hands on my head and in a fatherly way, he drew me to his chest. I smelled a strong perfume, as of roses. I thought to myself that this scent must come from the wound in his side. I wept with joy because of his paternal love and affection for me.

My brother kissed his hand as well, and Padre Pio wished us both a safe journey. Then we left for Pietrelcina.

Antonio was a tall and attractive young man who was encouraged by friends to go to Rome and seek a career in acting. In fact, he had already been accepted by an acting school and wanted to go. First, however, he went to Padre Pio for counsel. The Padre told him, "What! You want to become an actor so you can lose your soul?" Antonio changed his mind and dedicated himself to more academic studies.

I have another brother Mario Pio. He wanted to become a professional cyclist when he was 17 years old in 1956. He trained hard and won many races. My mother counseled him and told him to ask the Padre about his career choice. So, he cycled from Pietrelcina to San Giovanni Rotondo. This took many hours of grueling hills and winding turns.

Arriving at San Giovanni Rotondo, he went to Padre Pio for confession and told him, "Padre, I want to become a cyclist. I love bike racing." Padre Pio said, "No, because of hunger you will lose your sight." He meant that because of this passion of my brother's, he might lose his vision of things.

He listened to Padre Pio and put bike racing out of his mind. He never returned to San Giovanni Rotondo on a bicycle. In our family we never made major decisions without first asking for counsel from our spiritual father.

Another Counsel

My mother and I were in San Giovanni Rotondo in 1949. On the day prior to our departure, my mother told Padre Pio that we would be leaving the next day. Padre Pio told her, "No, tomorrow you must not leave." My mother said, "Very well then, we shall stay longer." We always listened to the Padre.

The following day we heard that the train we were scheduled to take from Foggia to Benevento had collided with another train with terrible consequences. We wondered what might have happened to us if we had taken that train as originally planned.

Our dear Padre had advised us before the accident. With tears in her eyes, my mother went to thank him. Whenever we departed from San Giovanni Rotondo, I always smelled a strong perfume, like a fragrant wind that came and went. At times like this, I would say to myself that the Padre is near and watching over us.

Giuseppe DeNunzio

Padre Pio was in Pietrelcina for about six years after his ordination because his poor health prevented his return to the Capuchin community. His superiors thought the native air would agree with him. Every morning he celebrated Mass. His Masses were always very long and the people who had to go to work would grow impatient.

While in Pietrelcina, everyone approached him for help in all matters. Zio Giuseppe DeNunzio, my uncle, recalled that as a boy, he suffered from paralysis of the legs, Padre Pio visited him and placed his hands on the powerless limbs with great compassion and prayer.

Padre Pio's Ordination

When Padre Pio was ordained in August 1910, he had to go to Benevento for the ordination. At that time there were no buses or cars, so, he went by horse and buggy. Padre Pio's mother, his parish priest and a few friends accompanied him. The driver of his vehicle was Alessandro Mandato, the grandfather of my husband Andre.

Padre Pio's first Mass was celebrated in the parish church of Pietrelcina, Our Lady of the Angels. The ceremony took place on the main altar of *La Madonna della Libera* on Sunday, August 14, 1910. There were great celebrations in Pietrelcina for our new priest. My father was 16 years old at the time and remembered the occasion well.

Testimony of My Cousin and Padre Pio's Parents

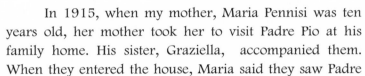

In 1915, when my mother, Maria Pennisi was ten years old, her mother took her to visit Padre Pio at his family home. His sister, Graziella, accompanied them. When they entered the house, Maria said they saw Padre Pio sitting on a bed wearing his Franciscan habit, and his face was like that of Jesus. Maria said, "He looked at us and gave us three holy cards. We will always remember his face looking like that of Jesus."

Maria also told us that Padre Pio's mother, Giuseppa DeNunzio Forgione, was a very good woman. In December 1928, Giuseppa wanted to be near her son at San Giovanni Rotondo and so she stayed with Mary Pyle.

Every morning she went to the friary, attended her son's Mass and received Holy Communion from his hands. She would, at times, come close to her son in order to kiss his hands like the others did, but Padre Pio would withdraw them from her. She became upset, and once, with tears in her eyes said, "I've been here twenty days, and I can't kiss your hands." Seeing her discomfort, Padre Pio said to his mother, "When is it ever seen that a mother has to kiss the hands of her son?" From that day on she no longer attempted to do so.

Because of the terrible cold, Giuseppa caught pneumonia and had a high fever that confined her to

bed. Padre Pio often went to visit her, and sitting by her bed with great emotion, administered the Sacrament of the Sick to her. When she died, he kissed her forehead and cried. In fact, he was so distraught that he could not return to the friary and stayed at Mary's home for several days. He kept repeating, "My mother, my beautiful mother, how much you loved me." Giuseppa DeNunzio Forgione died on the 3rd of January in 1929.

Orazio Forgione, the Padre's father, died on the 7th of October in 1946. He also stayed at Mary Pyle's house, while Padre Pio assisted him for four days and nights until he died. His father died in the same room, as did his mother. The Padre again suffered intensely, and cried over and over, "My father, my father." He was thinking about the sacrifices his father had made. He especially remembered his father going to the United States to make money so that he could attend seminary school.

My father met up with Padre Pio shortly after his father's death and found him grieving in the choir loft. My father came close to him and offered his condolences and those of the entire town.

Dedication of the Pietrelcina Convent

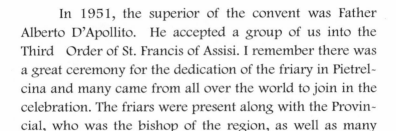

In 1951, the superior of the convent was Father Alberto D'Apollito. He accepted a group of us into the Third Order of St. Francis of Assisi. I remember there was a great ceremony for the dedication of the friary in Pietrelcina and many came from all over the world to join in the celebration. The friars were present along with the Provincial, who was the bishop of the region, as well as many others from San Giovanni Rotondo. Mary Pyle, the great benefactress of the friary, was also there.

I entered the church along with the Sisters of the Precious Blood. We felt raindrops and believed them to be Padre Pio's blessing, since he wanted to come but was unable to do so. The Mass was beautiful, but the joy was lessened because of the absence of the Padre.

A number of days after the dedication, Zio Mercurio and my father were telling Padre Pio about the dedication and how it would have been better if he had been there. The Padre told them, "But you don't know anything! You don't even know how many steps there are in front of the friary." He told them the exact number of steps.....nine. They were speechless because it was an accurate number. It was also the Padre's way of causing them to understand that he was present, through bilocation, for the ceremony. We felt this confirmed our feelings about the raindrops being a blessing given from the Padre.

A Cross in the Sky

When construction on the Church of the Holy Family began, the entire town of Pietrelcina was enthusiastic about the project and became actively involved. Both men and women volunteered their time to work, whether it meant gathering stones, mixing cement or doing anything else that was needed.

One night, a luminous cross appeared over the stones near the construction site. It was as high as the stars and remained immobile for half an hour, before it slowly rose and disappeared into the sky. The elderly continue to tell this story to the young, so that it will never be forgotten.

Padre Pio's Gift of Reading Hearts

A good friend of Padre Pio, Nicola La Banga, also from Pietrelcina, knew him as a young man. Nicola was a shoemaker. One night while Padre Pio was in San Giovanni Rotondo, Nicola experienced a terrible pain in his teeth and began to complain. He was barely able to speak.

In his bedroom a picture of the Padre hung on the wall. Nicola's wife said, "Nicola, invoke Padre Pio's name and pray, and you will get better." Nicola became angry, and while lying in bed he picked up a shoe and threw it at the picture of the Padre. He mumbled, "What! I have to invoke his name too!"

Close to a year passed, and Nicola found himself in San Giovanni Rotondo going to Padre Pio for confession. After confession, Padre Pio asked, "Nicola, what else do you have to tell me?" "Nothing else, Padre," he replied. Then the Padre said, "When you threw the shoe at my picture, did you think that you would be able to hit me all the way from Pietrelcina? Your teeth were hurting you and you took it out on me." Nicola turned pale, wondering how Padre Pio was able to know about something that had occurred a long while ago and from such a great distance.

My Grandfather ~ Antonio DeNunzio

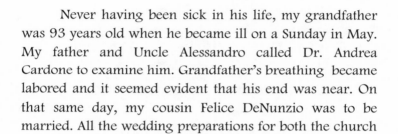

Never having been sick in his life, my grandfather was 93 years old when he became ill on a Sunday in May. My father and Uncle Alessandro called Dr. Andrea Cardone to examine him. Grandfather's breathing became labored and it seemed evident that his end was near. On that same day, my cousin Felice DeNunzio was to be married. All the wedding preparations for both the church ceremony and the home reception had been made well in advance.

That same morning at 8, Silvio Scocca came to visit us. He was the son of Zio Mercurio Scocca and had been baptized by Padre Pio. He asked if we had any messages for the Padre, since he was on his way to San Giovanni Rotondo. We explained the situation to him and asked him to tell the Padre to pray for our dying grandfather.

At 11 a.m. Silvio met Padre Pio and embraced him affectionately, saying, "this morning I was with Paris and he wants you to pray for his father, Antonio DeNunzio, who is dying. Also, today, the family is preparing for a wedding to take place." The Padre responded by saying, "I will pray."

At that exact moment, 11 a.m. in Pietrelcina, to the surprise of all of us, my grandfather sat up in bed.

He looked at each of us and seemed completely well. Even the doctor was amazed.

My cousin's wedding took place as planned. Throughout the five hours of celebration, my grandfather remained a part of the festivities, eating everything, even the sweets, even though he was confined to his bed.

When the wedding feast concluded, my grandfather died. We all thanked the Lord for this time of grace and we thanked Padre Pio for his help too.

Silvio Scocca

Silvio came to our house one morning and told us that he was on his way to visit Padre Pio. He sat down, while my mother gave him coffee and wrote a note for the Padre. She placed it in an envelope and gave it to Silvio to give to the Padre.

As soon as he arrived in San Giovanni Rotondo Silvio went to confession. When he was finished, Padre Pio asked him, "Do you have anything else to tell me?" "No, Padre," he replied. Padre Pio then told him, "This morning you went to visit Paris and Maria, and you had coffee with them. You are forgetting to give me Paris' greeting and the note Maria gave to you." "Oh, yes, Padre," responded the absent-minded Silvio, "here is the letter!" When he returned to Pietrelcina and told us what had happened, we marveled. Silvio said, "Padre Pio knew all the details of the note beforehand."

Another time when Silvio went to visit Padre Pio, a woman from Pietrelcina entrusted him with a box of candy to give to the Padre. Traveling by train, Silvio became very hungry and ate some of the candy but carefully rewrapped the package.

When he arrived in San Giovanni Rotondo and met with Padre Pio, the Padre asked, "Silvio, how was the train ride?" "It was good, Padre," he responded, then handed him the package of rewrapped candy. Padre Pio looked

at him and asked, "Silvio how many candies did you eat on the train?" Silvio didn't know what to say. He told us that one cannot hide anything from the Padre

Mercurio Scocca and
Padre Pio's Armchair

As was mentioned earlier, when Padre Pio lived in Pietrelcina he often stayed in the country, on his parents' little farm. There, in the middle of a field, he would sit on a rock that he called his *poltrona* or armchair. It was there that he read, studied and prayed.

Long after Padre Pio left Pietrelcina, Silvio Scocca decided to move the rock onto his own property. Using a long chain pulled by a horse, he tried to uproot it, but it wouldn't budge. After much effort he finally gave up.

When he visited Padre Pio sometime later and went to confession, the Padre asked him, "Silvio, what did you want to do with my *poltrona?* Did you want to take it? It will not be moved from its place!"

Silvio remained silent. This rock, which many have gone to see, is still in its original place in Piana Romana. It remains near the chapel that was constructed by the elm tree, where Padre Pio received the invisible stigmata in the fall of 1910. These wounds became visible in San Giovanni Rotondo on September 20, 1918 in front of a crucifix. They bled for half a century.

Padre Pio's Messages

When people from Pietrelcina went to visit the Padre, he would always ask, "What are my *paesani* doing?" Then he would add, "I have many times raised my hands in blessing and presented everyone to Jesus Christ and St. Francis."

During World War II the Germans came through Pietrelcina and everyone was worried. Some people went to the Padre for words of comfort. He told them, "Be tranquil. Pietrelcina will be protected like the pupils of my eyes." The next day the soldiers moved out.

Padre Pio was often heard saying, "Pietrelcina is totally in my heart." Although he lived 52 years in San Giovanni Rotondo he remained tied to his native town. Once he said, "In Pietrelcina, Jesus came and everything happened there."

PART THREE

Under Padre Pio's Guidance

San Giovanni Rotondo Again

After a visit with Padre Pio, I always left with a special feeling. The memory of his visit and his presence, remained with me for a long time. Whenever I thought of him, I felt protected and secure. To me he was both a father and a mother, and I ran to him for advice on many matters.

One day I wasn't feeling well. I was suffering from stomach pains and I told him of my problem. "My daughter," he replied, "what do you want to do, go to heaven with sandals on?" He meant that suffering is a part of life and in order to enter heaven, one must bear one's cross with courage.

There were numerous times when many people would gather around him as he passed by and they would shout out loud, "Padre, I have a sick son," or, "Padre, my husband is ill. Help me!" Padre Pio would usually respond, "You pray, and I will pray."

I remember the many women I got to know who attended his Masses at San Giovanni Rotondo. I noticed that when the Padre ended his Mass and left the altar with his hands uncovered, revealing his wounds, women would go and pick up the scabs that had fallen from his hands. I, too, joined them and picked up those precious relics.

Testimony of Ettore Masone

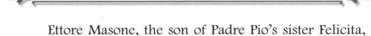

Ettore Masone, the son of Padre Pio's sister Felicita, lived at Mary Pyle's house. We often went together to visit friends from Pietrelcina, and he would often speak of his uncle. His nickname was Ettoruccio, Little Hector, and he had the privilege of being baptized by his uncle.

Ettoruccio told me that when he was young, Padre Pio had to be operated on for a cyst. The doctor performed the minor surgery in the friary. Naturally, no one was allowed in the room, but Ettoruccio hid himself and quietly watched. He heard his uncle speaking and joking with the doctor.

When the procedure was finished, Ettoruccio came out of hiding and asked the doctor to check his tonsils, since they were causing him pain. During this examination, Padre Pio, with his great sense of humor, began to tease him. "Ettore," he said, "Where were you hiding? Look at this, he slips into places to hide!" Padre Pio had a great affection for his adventurous nephew.

Ettoruccio's Aunt Graziella, another sister of Padre Pio, eventually became a nun in the Order of St. Bridget and was called Sister Pia. The Padre accompanied her to Rome in 1913 when she entered the convent.

Soon after, Padre Pio left Pietrelcina for the last time, Ettoruccio's mother died on September 23rd in 1918.

Exactly fifty years prior to the day of her famous brother.

When his sister died, Padre Pio had only just received the visible wounds of Christ. Although he was in bed with a high fever and in great pain, he managed to write a letter of comfort to his parents. Ettoruccio's father was Vincenzo Masone, who was a cousin of my future mother-in-law, Angela Masone Mandato

Padre Pio Chooses My Husband

There were three young men who expressed an interest in me and who wanted to explore the possibility of marriage.

When I was 19 years old, one young man became interested in me, but I would not respond to him until I first spoke with Padre Pio. I went to confession and told him of this young man. He was a teacher and seemed to be a good person. Padre Pio listened and then asked, "How do you know what clothes he wears?"

I wondered what he meant by those words. So, my father decided to look into the young man's background and discovered that he was a communist. He carried a communist card and wore the emblem of the party. Also, he was not a Catholic. My mother said, "This is what Padre Pio meant by his words." Soon after, I told him I wasn't interested in seeing him again.

Another time during confession, my mother told the Padre that there was a second young man interested in me. This time he was a Catholic and came from a good family. Which man would Padre Pio advise me to marry? The Padre responded, "No, it is still early for Graziella." My mother then said, "But, Padre, she is twenty-one years old." "No," the Padre said, "she is still twenty."

On another occasion, a man from San Giovanni

Rotondo pursued me. He wanted to meet my parents and get to know them. I told him I needed some time to think about it. Since I was in San Giovanni Rotondo, I was able to speak about it with the Padre. After confession, I very shyly told him about it. Padre Pio began to laugh and said, "You don't want to settle here on this mountain."

By these words I understood that this young man was not intended for me either, nor did the Padre believe I would settle in San Giovanni Rotondo. I would have enjoyed remaining there, as some from Pietrelcina had done. For instance, Padre Pio's niece, Pia Forgione, married a man from San Giovanni Rotondo and settled there just to be near her uncle.

A number of years later in 1953, Padre Pio chose my future husband. Andre Mandato, was from Pietrelcina and had moved to Bologna to open a tailor's shop. Since we were both from the same town, we already knew each other.

Andre asked me to marry him. I told him that I needed time to think. Without telling him, I decided to go a second time to my spiritual father for advice about my future. Andre wanted a response by August of that year. This was when he planned to visit Pietrelcina.

In May of the same year I went with my mother to Padre Pio for confession. I said, "Padre, I am in need of your help and counsel regarding the choice of a husband." Padre Pio listened attentively and said, "Good, tell me whom you are thinking about?" I told him of the first young man. Padre Pio asked, "Who else?" I told him of the second and again the Padre asked, "Who else?" "Andre Mandato," I replied. He said, "Certainly, a good artist. The angel of God has passed by. Marry with the Lord's blessing. Amen."

I kissed his hand and went to sit directly in front of him as he continued to hear confessions I watched him and thought about what he had said: "Andre is a good artist (tailor)." I didn't expect Andre as the Padre's choice because I still preferred the first young man.

I wanted to discuss this matter with my mother, but she and many others were waiting for the Padre to hear her confession. I decided to wait until we could talk outside.

My mother suddenly noticed Padre Pio motioning her to come to him.. She thought he was motioning to someone else, but again he repeated the gesture. She then went to him, knelt directly in front of the confessional and confessed face-to-face Since she didn't have to wait on line, she was quite content and became aware of the scent of roses.

We went outside after we received Holy Communion from the Padre, since my mother wanted to know what he told me. I answered, "Padre Pio told me to marry Andre." She picked up on my disappointment and said, "You have to listen to what the Padre says. He is your spiritual father and you must obey."

In August 1953, when Andre Mandato returned to Pietrelcina, he wanted to know my answer. I told him that I had spoken to Padre Pio about him. Andre was happily surprised, since he never thought that I would consult the Padre about this matter. He was deeply moved that Padre Pio had chosen him with the blessing of the Lord.

We became engaged and I told Andre that if he wanted to please me, he had to go to Padre Pio for confession and ask to be accepted as a spiritual son. "Yes, to please you, I will do this," he replied. After several days he went along with my father to visit the Padre.

While Padre Pio was hearing his confession, he asked to be accepted as a spiritual son. Padre Pio replied, "Yes, but behave well." Andre began to have a great devotion to him as well.

After a two-year engagement, Andre and I accompanied my father on a visit to Padre Pio. Andre asked the Padre when we should get should get married. The Padre replied, "Quickly, for I don't like things to drag on."

After we were married, in August 1955, Uncle Alessandro DeNunzio died. We believe his death was the reason why Padre Pio told us to marry quickly. Otherwise, there would have been a death in the family and the marriage would have had to be postponed.

Our Nuptials

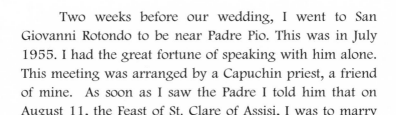

Two weeks before our wedding, I went to San Giovanni Rotondo to be near Padre Pio. This was in July 1955. I had the great fortune of speaking with him alone. This meeting was arranged by a Capuchin priest, a friend of mine. As soon as I saw the Padre I told him that on August 11, the Feast of St. Clare of Assisi, I was to marry Andre in Pietrelcina.

"Padre, I want a memory from you on that day," I told him. He replied, "Very well, I will tell Padre Carmelo to send you a telegram. This way I will send you my best wishes and a special blessing." I said, "Thank you, Padre, then after the wedding we shall come here to see you." "Certainly," he responded, "you have to come so both of you can receive a blessing."

"Padre," I added, "after we are married, I have to go and live in Bologna. I must leave my family for a new place. Pray for me." He said, "Very well, I will remain close to you." "Grazie, Padruccio," I contentedly replied. He touched my head and wished me well for my upcoming wedding. I heard Padre Pio whisper *my daughter*, and I again smelled the familiar scent of roses.

Andre and I were married on August 11, 1955 by the local pastor in the beautiful church of Our Lady of the Angels. This is the same church where I was baptized and

where Padre Pio celebrated his first Mass. The church is just one street away from where I lived with my parents.

I wanted Padre Pio to marry us, but we couldn't travel to San Giovanni Rotondo because Andre's father was not well. Instead, on our wedding day we received a telegram from Padre Carmelo De Sassano, on behalf of Padre Pio saying, "To the newlyweds, Graziella and Andre, Padre Pio wishes you a long and holy life. He sends you his humble blessing."

We received another telegram from my husband's Aunt Rosinella Mandato, who lived in San Giovanni Rotondo, with further blessings and prayers from Padre Pio. That night I dreamed Padre Pio gave me Holy Communion and allowed me to kiss his hand. He showed me just how close he would remain with me.

Married Life

The day after our wedding we left for San Giovanni Rotondo, where the friars had arranged a meeting for both of us with Padre Pio. We met him at the altar and received Communion from him. Afterwards, he told us, "Congratulations to you. Be happy. Love each other and form a beautiful Christian family." He touched our hands and we each kissed his hand.

We experienced tremendous joy when his beautiful eyes gazed upon us, showing us his paternal affection. We were filled with the wonderful scent of roses and I wept like a child.

Afterwards, we gathered outside. Many of the townspeople came to congratulate us, including Aunt Rosinella and my godmother Pia, who invited us to her home. We visited with her and her husband Mario for a while.

We also went on to visit Mary Pyle, who embraced us with affection and gave us a gift. It was a rather large, framed portrait of Padre Pio celebrating Mass. We later had Padre Pio bless it and we continue to cherish the beautiful memory it invokes.

Soon after, I accompanied my new husband to Bologna. We lived in the center of this big, medieval city and I liked it very much. There were lovely churches which

I visited everyday.

In October 1955, I learned that I was pregnant and was excited at the thought of becoming a mother. The following February, in 1956, my father and I went to San Giovanni Rotondo. I had a tremendous desire to see the Padre.

When we arrived and entered the church, he was already hearing women's confessions. Since his confessional was open in the front, he could look out and see people as they entered. I sat near him and began to pray. I knew I couldn't go to confession, due to the fact that one needed to reserve a spot days in advance. Many people from all over Italy, and the world, came to receive the Sacrament of Penance from him, and there was not enough time to accommodate all of them without a reservation. So, I simply looked at him while his eyes remained fixed on me. I was inwardly moved. Was he reading my thoughts once again?

Somehow, I received the courage to go toward his confessional without a ticket. The woman who was at the head of the long line and next to see the Padre, let me go in her place. As I entered the confessional, Padre Pellegrino immediately arrived. He was responsible for checking tickets and maintaining order on the confessional line. Padre Pellegrino approached Padre Pio and said, "Padre, Graziella entered the confessional without a reservation," to which Padre Pio replied, "And when she did, who were you watching?"

I made my confession and afterward knelt in front

of him and told him I was pregnant. "Padre, what name should I give my child?" "Call him Pio Francesco," he replied. I kissed his hand and he blessed me. I returned and sat by his confessional and waited to receive Holy Communion.

I was very happy to know that I would give birth to a boy and that I should name him Pio Francesco. On July 6, 1956, the Feast of Saint Maria Goretti, Pio Francesco was born.

My Aunt Rosinella went to the Padre and told him that her niece had given birth to a son and that the baby had been given the name of Pio Francesco. Padre Pio sent his greetings and blessings for little Pio and me. He also sent along a little medal for the newborn, with the image of Our Lady on one side and St. Michael on the other. My aunt sent this to me as quickly as she could.

Padre Pio Meets Pio Francesco and the Birth of Another Son

In August 1960, when Pio was four years old, we went to visit Padre Pio. My father went with us. He took his grandson to the Padre's room, where there were other friars. After Pio kissed the Padre's hand, Padre Pio asked the boy, "What is your name?" "I'm Pio Francesco," the boy replied. Padre Pio said, "Bravo! Bravo!" He embraced Pio and pulled him to himself and blessed him. Afterward, Pio told his grandfather that a beautiful perfume came from the Padre's tummy.

During Easter, 1956, I received a letter from Angelina de Stefano. I had stayed with her while I was in San Giovanni Rotondo between 1947 and 1955. She went to Padre Pio and asked him to send me some counsel. He replied, "May she imitate Jesus crucified, live for Him in order to rise with Him for eternal glory." What beautiful words Padre Pio sent me that Easter.

While living in Bologna, we took off every August and went south to Pietrelcina to visit family and friends and to celebrate the feast of the *Madonna della Libera,* the patron saint of Pietrelcina. The journey to Pietrelcina took eight hours by train. Of course, I always went on to visit with the Padre at San Giovanni Rotondo.

In August 1957, I went with my father to visit the Padre, while my husband remained in Pietrelcina with our

son Pio Francesco. Soon after arriving in San Giovanni Rotondo, I had the opportunity to let Padre Pio hear my confession.

After receiving absolution, I went before him and said, "Padre, I am pregnant again and would like to know the name I should give my child." He replied, "Give him your father-in-law's name, Vincenzo." I said, "Very good," remembering that my father-in-law was displeased that we did not name our first-born after him. We believe that Padre Pio had the gift of understanding this situation without ever being told.

On December 23, 1957, I went shopping in Bologna with Andre and young Pio Francesco. The sidewalk was very wet and I slipped. I was nine months pregnant. I avoided falling on my stomach by landing on my hand, but I dislocated my wrist and the pain was intense. However, I did not want to get it checked since I was due to give birth and I did not want a cast on my hand. I invoked Padre Pio and said, "Now, you must help me." In a short time, my wrist felt better.

On December 24th, my mother arrived from Pietrelcina, after having traveled all night by train. That Christmas Eve we prepared a festive meal. Before we could enjoy it, I went into labor. My husband said, "What a beautiful Christmas Eve. We can't even eat!" We took a cab to the hospital where I spent the entire night in labor.

By Christmas morning our second son was born. We named him Vincenzo because Padre Pio advised us to do so

However, since he was born on Christmas Day we gave him Nazzareno as his middle name, after Jesus of Nazareth. The doctors and nurses came to congratulate me and gave me a small statue of the Baby Jesus.

On December 26, St. Stephen's Day, a telegram arrived from San Giovanni Rotondo with the words: "A little gift for the newborn. Greetings from Padre Pio." It was signed by Padre Carmelo. I have kept this letter as one of my many mementos. Again, we had not had the time to inform Padre Pio of Vincenzo's birth, but through his gift of prophecy he already knew.

Salvatore Scigliuzzi's Story

In Bologna there were many people devoted to Padre Pio. One day Salvatore Scigliuzzi and his wife, Germana, came to visit us. They had been in San Giovanni Rotondo and happened to meet up with my father, who told them that I was now living in Bologna. They were pleased to find us living there.

Salvatore lost his sight after the Second World War as the result of an illness. Often he and his wife visited Padre. Pio. They had three sons. Their youngest son Albert received his First Holy Communion from the Padre's wounded hands on the 11th of August in 1958.

Albert once asked the Padre about his father's blindness. "Padre," he said, "you are able to perform so many miracles. Why can't you obtain the grace for my father so he can see?" Padre Pio looked at him and said, "Ask your father. He didn't want the grace."

Albert went to his parents and told them that he had spoken with the Padre. "I asked for the grace of your sight, but he told me to ask you about it," Albert said. The father began to weep and said, "It's true. I said, no, to the Padre because I heard a voice inside me that said I should offer up my blindness to Jesus."

Sometime later during a visit to San Giovanni Rotondo, Salvatore was in a crowd of people waiting to

go to confession. Noticing him, Padre Pio came down the stairs that led into the church and approached Salvatore. The Padre looked at him, and for a few moments Salvatore was able to see Padre Pio's face clearly. Then the Padre tenderly touched Salvatore's eyes. Salvatore was deeply moved that Padre Pio allowed himself to be seen, even for such a brief moment.

Salvatore offered up his blindness and it had a powerful effect on the city in which he lived. There were many communists in his city, and many of them knew him. They were touched by Salvatore's faith and peace, but they were especially moved by the serenity with which he accepted his loss of sight.

He organized many religious groups which resulted in lives being changed for the better. He brought many men to San Giovanni Rotondo to Padre Pio. In Bologna, Salvatore and his wife were frequent visitors to our home. He even became godfather to our third boy, Paolo Paris.

Birth of My Third Son

In 1961, I was pregnant for the third time. I often visited a nearby church and attended daily Mass. Afterwards, I would light a candle before a beautiful statue of Our Lady portrayed as a young girl. Since we already had two boys, I prayed for the birth of a daughter.

In July of that year, six months before the birth of my child, I had a dream about Padre Pio. In it he said, "Graziella, resign yourself for the child to be born will also be a boy. You will call him Pietro." I quickly awoke and told my husband about the dream. I then resigned myself to the Lord's will.

On December 15, 1961, I gave birth to a boy and we named him Paolo Paris. This was the only time that I didn't listen to Padre Pio. Our friends Salvatore and Germana Scigliuzzi wanted us to name our son Paolo, since they too had a son named Paolo. We added the name Paris in honor of my father.

Once Padre Pio asked my father, "Paris, why don't you change your name? What kind of a name is it, a French name?" My father said, "Padre, this is the name they gave me." Padre Pio simply smiled.

Laurentana Carretti

Laurentana Carretti, a schoolteacher from Bologna, had a great love for my family and me and a special fondness for Pio Francesco. Once, Padre Pio appeared to her through bilocation.

In 1948, she became so ill that she remained bedridden, unable to move and no longer able to teach. Since she was devoted to Padre Pio, she prayed to him for his intercession and asked for a healing. One day Padre Pio appeared to her in her bedroom, through bilocation. As she lay in her bed, he drew close to her and touched her shoulder with his hand. Then he said to her, "You will be healed. You will be healed," and disappeared.

Laurentana was surprised and overjoyed at having seen Padre Pio. She called to her husband from another room, and in a loud voice exclaimed, "Come quickly, for I have seen Padre Pio." "It's impossible," her husband said. "No, you have to believe me. Padre Pio touched my shoulder," she responded. Her husband looked and noticed drops of fresh blood on her nightgown. He couldn't believe it and remarked, "This is a miracle. Padre Pio has been in our house through bilocation."

Laurentana was healed and there remained an aroma of perfume in the room. She put the piece of blood-stained cloth inside a gold medallion and wore it around

her neck for many years. Eventually, she bought a glass encasement in which she placed the gold medallion. She kept it as a relic, believing that the blood came from the Padre's wounded hands. In 1968, when she was 75 years old, she prayed to Padre Pio and asked him what she should ultimately do with the medallion. She considered this to be her greatest treasure. Padre Pio came to her in a dream and said, "Leave the medallion to Graziella."

While living in the United States, I received a letter from Laurentana recounting the entire experience. My brother Pio, who was then living in Bologna, picked up the relic from her house to give to me. Now, I have this beautiful treasure of hers, which I keep with great devotion.

Thank you Padre Pio!

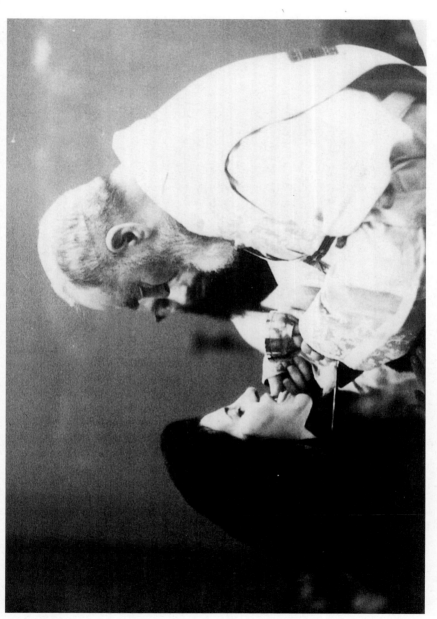

Graziella receiving the Holy Eucharist from Padre Pio, 1964.

Grazio Forgione, Padre Pio's Father, 1952

Giuseppa DeNunzio Forgione, Padre Pio's Mother, 1924
Courtesy: Abresch Federico Photographers, San Giovanni Rotondo

The House in Pietrelcina where Padre Pio was born on May 25, 1887.

Early photo of Padre Pio showing stigmata.
Courtesy: Church of S. Maria degli Angeli

The trunk of the preserved elm tree:

-witnesses to the extraordinary phenomena that took place on the Piana Romana;

-and marvels worked by our Lord in His servant Padre Pio.

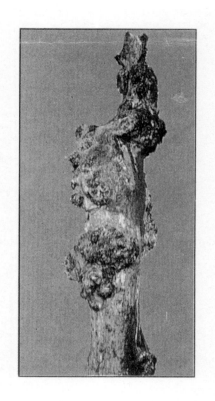

* * *

"Many times I raised my hand, in the silence of the night and refuge of my cell, to bless you all."

Padre Pio

Courtesy: Capuchin Friary, Pietrelcina, Italy

Elm tree trunk now enclosed to protect it from relic seekers.

Church In Piana Romana constructed alongside the elm tree trunk. To the left is the well where the young Francesco Forgione told his father to dig for water.

Interior view of the same church showing the chapel of Saint Francis.

*Graziella in front of the Capuchin Convent
San Giovanni Rotondo, 1950.*

The second rosary given to Graziella by Padre Pio.

Graziella with her brother Antonio and to their right,
Etteruccio Masone and a friend in San Giovanni Rotondo, 1955.

Corso Padre Pio, Pietrelcina

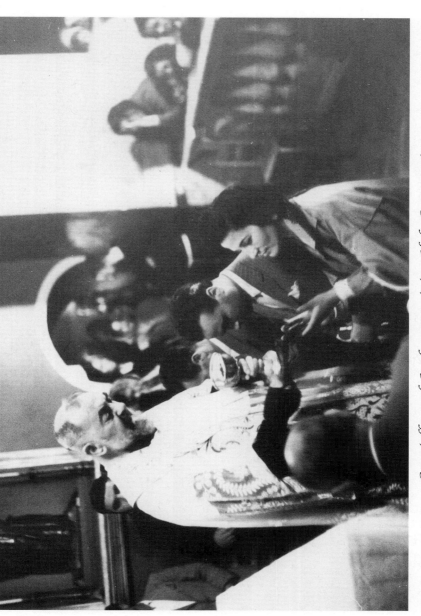

Graziella and Andrea receiving Holy Communion from Padre Pio after their marriage, 1955.

Padre Pio blesses Graziella and Andrea. Touching their heads with his wounded hands, he congratulates and wishes them well

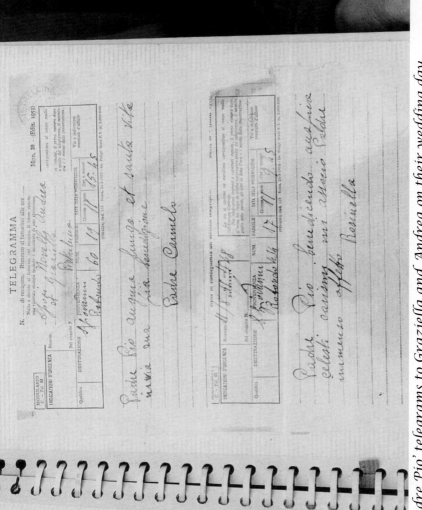

Padre Pío' telegrams to Graziella and Andrea on their wedding day, wishing them celestial blessings and many gifts of the spirit.

Padre Pio with his brother, Michele Forgione,
San Giovanni Rotondo, 1958.

Salvatore Scigliuzzi, the blind man who was blessed by Padre Pio and was enabled to see Padre Pio's face for a few seconds, 1958.

Graziella's sons Pio Francesco and Vincenzo Mandato receiving their First Holy Communion from Padre Pio, 1964.

Pio Francesco and Vincenzo Mandato the day of their
First Holy Communion, San Giovanni Rotondo, 1964

Aunt Rosinella Mandato and Padre Alessio Parente, 1965

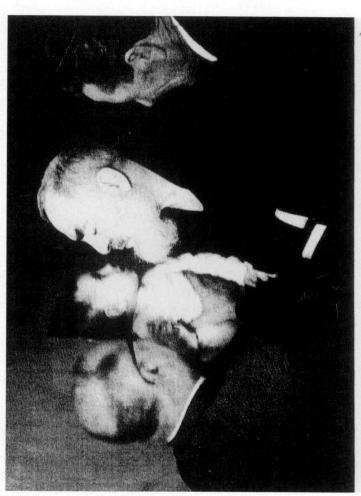

PARIS·DE·NUNZIO

Paris DeNunzio looks on as Padre Pio kisses a child, 1966

Padre Pio joking with Graziella's father Paris DeNunzio, and to their right, other childhood friends, Antonio Sagliocca and Mercurio Scocca, 1966.

Padre Pio with Paris DeNunzio and to their right,
Padre Alessio Parente and Mercurio Scocca, 1967

The Church of the Holy Family and the Convent of the Capuchin Fathers

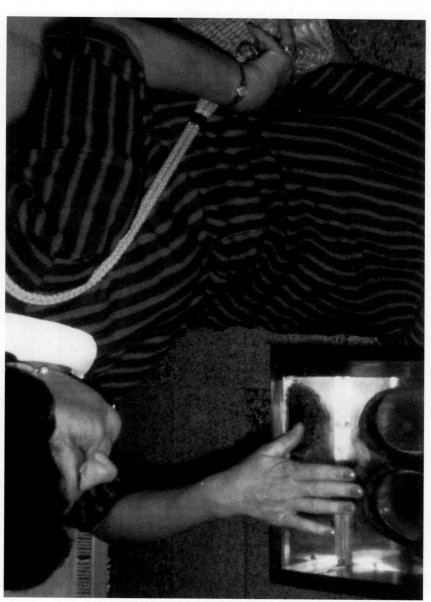

Graziella gazes emotionally at the sandals worn by Padre Pio, 1983.

Father Pio Francesco Mandato celebrating his first Mass in the Church of Santa Maria degli Angeli, 1985

Father Pio Francesco Mandato with his maternal grandparents, Paris DeNunzio and Maria Pennisi in the Church of S. Maria degli Angeli, on the day of his first Mass, 1985.

Graziella and Father Pio Francesco with the statue of La Madonna della Libera. Photo taken while the Church of Santa Maria degli Angeli was undergoing restoration, 1986.

La Madonna della Libera being carried in procession from the Church of Santa Maria degli Angeli, Pietrelcina, 1987.

Fr. Pio FrancescoMandato celebrates Mass in 1995 at the altar where Padre Pio celebrated his first Holy Mass in 1910.

Graziella DeNunzio Mandato with her husband Andrea and their family.

"I have raised my hand high many times in the silence of
the night and the privacy of my cell, blessing you all."
Padre Pio

Courtesy: The Capuchin Friars Minor, Pietrelcina.

The Healing of My Son, Pio

In 1962, our son Pio became ill. He developed an infection around his mouth and ran a high fever. Even though the doctor gave him medication, his condition did not improve. My Aunt Rosinella happened to be visiting her family in Pietrelcina. She ran into my mother who informed her that Pio was not well.

When she returned to San Giovanni Rotondo, she went to see Padre Pio and asked him to pray for my son. Padre Pio replied, "Well, what can we do? Let us give thanks to the Lord that all has passed. Let's send them a paternal benediction."

As soon as I received my aunt's letter with the news of Padre Pio's words, my son became completely healed. The Padre had prayed for Pio and his prayers were answered.

My Sons' First Communion and
Our Move to the United States

My husband Andre was invited to work as a specialized tailor in a factory owned by my uncle Umberto Pennisi, in New York City. Andre accepted the invitation and we decided to immigrate to the United States. In May 1964, my husband left for the United States to prepare a home for us, while I temporarily moved back to Pietrelcina. We intended to follow him within five months.

I wanted my two older sons, Pio and Vincent, now almost eight and seven, to receive their First Holy Communion from the hands of Padre Pio. I spoke to the Capuchin friars in Pietrelcina who immediately set up a date with the Capuchin friars in San Giovanni Rotondo.

My sons were prepared in Catholic doctrine by the same woman, Graziella Pannullo, who taught me when I was a young girl. Lucia Iadanza assisted her. Both women, who were dear friends of the Padre's, loved my children.

My parents, my brother Mario, my children and I all left for San Giovanni Rotondo. On October 3, 1964, Padre Pio celebrated Mass at 5 a.m. It was the Transitus of Saint Francis of Assisi, the celebration of his death. The friars prepared seats in the sanctuary of the church for my family. After my sons received their First Holy Communion from the hands of Padre Pio, the rest of us received as well.

After Mass, he approached the children and said, "Congratulations, boys. Always follow the way of the Lord, and may your last Communion be more beautiful than your first."

I cried and was filled with gratitude. I thanked the Lord for this beautiful gift that my sons had received from Padre Pio. Padre Vincent, a Capuchin of the friary who had a fondness for our family, invited us to meet with Padre Pio again.

We were in the hallway and I was holding two-year-old Paolo Paris in my arms. Then I said to Padre Pio, "Padre, this is my third child." He blessed him, caressed his face and gave each of the boys a little medal. Then I told him, "Padre, this month we are leaving for America. Will you bless us?" He blessed us saying, "Our Lady will accompany you." My father then asked him, "Padre, how do you counsel them to travel, by airplane or ship?" He replied, "By airplane."

I thought then of my husband, Andre, who was already in the United States and could not be present for our sons' First Holy Communion. I told my father, when he went upstairs to visit the Padre in his room, to ask for a pair of rosary beads for my husband. My father did as I asked and Padre Pio gave him rosary beads for Andre.

Arrival in the United States

Our journey from Rome to New York's Kennedy Airport went well. My husband had already begun his work as a tailor and had found an apartment for us in New Jersey.

I told Andre that Pio and Vincenzo had received their First Holy Communion from Padre Pio. He was overjoyed to hear about this. Then he reflected that both boys had benefited from the gift that was Padre Pio, but Paolo Paris would not have the same opportunity,

Soon afterwards, my husband dreamed of Padre Pio holding Paolo Paris in his arms. My youngest was three at the time. In the dream, Padre Pio approached Andre and requested to hold Paolo. He said, "Give me this boy. I will take him with me upstairs. Your other boys have received much from me, but Paolo Paris has not." Reflecting upon this dream, Andre understood that the Padre knew of his concern and was reassuring him that Paolo was also under his protection

After my arrival in the United States, the first few months were very difficult ones for me. I missed my family, and I didn't speak English. Above all, I missed Padre Pio. I called my father and asked if he would go to the Padre to request a blessing for me. Soon afterward when he was able to go and ask him, the Padre again asked, "How many times do I have to bless her?"

Christmas of that same year, my Aunt Rosinella told Padre Pio that she was planning to write me and inquired if he had any message for me. He replied, "Tell her that I bless her with all my heart. May Jesus, along with the Heavenly Mother, assist her and all her family." I was fortunate that my father and my aunt could send me greetings from the Padre.

In 1966, I received another letter from my Aunt Rosinella. She mentioned that her godson, Padre Alessio Parente and another friar who lived with Padre Pio, often visited her when they had some free time. He told her that he and Padre Pellegrino were taking care of Padre Pio and were with him constantly. This was two years before his death, and the Padre was suffering terribly. He could no longer stand on his wounded feet and would tire very easily.

During one of Padre Alessio's visits with Aunt Rosinella, he asked her if she was in need of anything. My Aunt replied, "Yes, I have to write my niece Graziella in America to wish her a happy Easter. Ask Padre Pio for some words and a blessing for her."

Padre Alessio went to the Padre and put the request before him. The Padre said, "Tell Graziella that I always have her present in my prayers and I am united to her whole family." Then he added, "Tell her to always keep herself good, holy, in union with her husband and in the Lord." My aunt added, "I hope you are happy with the words the Padre has sent you." I was thousands of miles away in another county, but my spiritual father was still

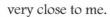

very close to me.

In May 1967, Padre Pio's brother Michele died. My father wrote to tell us, since he knew I had a great affection for Michele. Michele was always one of the frequent visitors in our home and I have many fond memories of him.

During the funeral Mass held in the Church of Our Lady of Grace in San Giovanni Rotondo, Padre Pio sat in the choir loft. After Mass, my father approached the Padre to express his condolences and those of the people of Pietrelcina. The Padre's eyes filled with tears and he expressed his gratitude.

Shortly after this sad event, my father went with his good friend, Zio Mercurio Scocca, to visit Padre Pio again. The Padre was content to see them again and said, "Look who is here. Come into my room so we can talk." On entering the room, Padre Pio sat down as my father knelt beside him to show him a picture of my three boys. The Padre looked at them and blessed them. Zio Mercurio, as always, spoke of Pietrelcina and Padre Pio's spirits rose. Zio Mercurio died in 1968 at the age of 81 in Pietrelcina, the same year that Padre Pio died.

March 1968

In March 1968, I wrote a letter to Padre Pio. However, I sent it to my father and had him personally bring it to my *Padruccio.* The letter read: "Dear Padre Pio, we have been living in an apartment for four years. We would like to buy a home and we are relying on your prayers so that all turns out well."

When the letter was presented to him, Padre Pio read it, blessed it and said to my father, "Send this back to your daughter." My father mailed me the letter, which I have kept as a remembrance. Two years later, in 1970, we found a lovely house on a nice piece of property in North Plainfield, New Jersey. Everything, indeed, turned out well.

Soon after we moved into the house we smelled a beautiful fragrance, the same fragrance that was common around Padre Pio. It was his way of showing us that he remained close to us. This made me feel very protected and at peace.

Padre Pio's Death

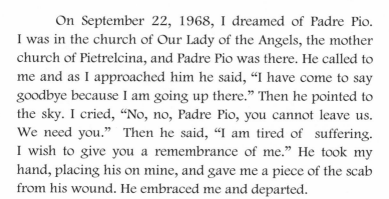

On September 22, 1968, I dreamed of Padre Pio. I was in the church of Our Lady of the Angels, the mother church of Pietrelcina, and Padre Pio was there. He called to me and as I approached him he said, "I have come to say goodbye because I am going up there." Then he pointed to the sky. I cried, "No, no, Padre Pio, you cannot leave us. We need you." Then he said, "I am tired of suffering. I wish to give you a remembrance of me." He took my hand, placing his on mine, and gave me a piece of the scab from his wound. He embraced me and departed.

Then I dreamed that I quickly went to my mother and told her that I had seen Padre Pio in church and showed her what he had given me. As I opened my hand, blood flowed out. She said, "That is a sign of blessings." When I awoke, I recounted everything for Andre. Together we tried to figure out the meaning of this dream, but it puzzled us. Perhaps, we didn't want to understand it.

Later, I turned on the radio to the Italian station, just as they were announcing that Padre Pio of Pietrelcina had died. This was September 23, 1968. I could not believe it. I suffered intensely and wept copiously saying, "My dear little father, my spiritual father has left us." My husband tried to console me.

Then I recalled another spiritual daughter of the Padre who once asked him, "Padre, when you are no longer here after your death, will you continue to assist us?" He responded simply, "If I have helped you in life, how much more will I help you after death?"

I was encouraged by this thought, for I knew that in Heaven he would be even closer to me. In fact, since his death, and up to the present time, he has visited me in dreams, offering me consolation and help in difficult moments.

Note: A relic pertains to the corpse of a saint or any part thereof; any part of his clothing; any thing intimately connected with him. Explanation taken from *A Catholic Dictionary* , published by Tan Press, 1997, p.423.

Padre Pio's Protection

During the night of June 12, 1972, I dreamed of Padre Pio. I was in church with the Padre when he took my hand and said, "Come with me. Kneel down, and let us pray together." I knelt by him and we prayed. He blessed me and I awoke. The following morning I went to Mass. It was the Feast of St. Anthony.

That afternoon I was driving my car. My son Pio was with me. We were crossing an intersection and a young man, driving rapidly, failed to stop at the stop sign. I veered to the right and he hit us. The car was totaled and we were taken to the hospital. Thank God, we were unharmed. I thanked the Lord for Padre Pio's prayerful intercession, for he showed us just how carefully we were protected.

Many years ago, I dreamed of Padre Pio telling me, "Graziella, you have to dedicate yourself more to praying before the Blessed Sacrament." The Padre was correct. I had many devotions to Our Lady and the saints but few to the Blessed Sacrament. I realized that Padre Pio knew everything, even how I prayed.

Padre Pio Helps Andre Stop Smoking

I once had a dream in which Padre Pio spoke of Andre's smoking habit. He told me, "Graziella, tell your husband Andre that if he wants to live, he must put cigarettes aside and stop smoking."

On awakening, I told my husband, but he refused to believe me. Then I said to him, "You may believe what you wish, but what I told you is what Padre Pio said."

One week later, to my astonishment, my husband stopped smoking. Padre Pio helped him quit. In fact, when he went for a physical, the doctor was happily surprised that he had stopped. He told Andre that his lungs were clean, amazingly better than they were before. My husband thanked the Padre for his warning and his help.

His Continued Guidance

In 1973, Padre Pio spoke to me in a dream, "Graziella, what a joy it is to see your sons, Pio Francesco and Vincenzo, serving Mass." I was very happy when I awoke. It was true! Pio and Vincent had been altar boys for a number of months.

The same happened with Paolo Paris. In my dream, the Padre approached us while we were seated in church and invited Paolo to accompany him to the altar to serve Mass. At the time Paolo Paris was an altar boy as well.

Graziella

In 1974, my father wrote me a letter that said my mother was suffering intensely from colitis. Her blood pressure was low and she battled with fevers. My very concerned father began to pray to Padre Pio and even placed a picture of the Padre on my mother. She quickly sensed Padre Pio's presence and felt his touch. The pain instantly disappeared. Both gave thanks to Padre Pio.

In 1975, my three sons and I returned to Italy for the first time since our move to the United States. In Pietrelcina, Padre Lino Barbati, the superior of the friary and a good friend, greeted me warmly and persuaded me to go to San Giovanni Rotondo. Accompanied by my parents, we traveled to San Giovanni Rotondo. While praying at the tomb of Padre Pio, I thanked him for all of his favors. We all smelled the lovely fragrance coming from his sanctified body. Through this sign, the Padre allowed us to understand that he continued to offer his protection.

Returning to San Giovanni Rotondo on Our 25th Wedding Anniversary

On our twenty-fifth wedding anniversary, in August of 1980, we went to Italy to celebrate in the town where we were married. Only our youngest son came with us. We had a Mass said in the Capuchin's Holy Family Church, celebrated by Padres Gianrico Tanno and Mario Mancanelli. We renewed our vows among family and friends.

The following day we traveled to San Giovanni Rotondo and by late morning we were praying at the Padre's tomb. All was silent and we were enveloped by a powerful peace.

Suddenly, I heard my name being called. Thinking it was my husband, I turned to him because he was kneeling beside me. However, he was praying and said that he had not called me. I then turned to my son and realized it couldn't have been him, since he would have called me 'Mom.' I realized it must have been Padre Pio letting me know he was near.

My husband soon turned to me and said, "Let us go attend Mass. It's the last Mass of the day." He, too, felt inspired by Padre Pio and heard him saying, "Andre, Andre, go to Mass. It's the last Mass of the day; otherwise, you will miss it."   We went upstairs to the big church and, indeed, it was the last Mass. In San Giovanni Rotondo there are daily Masses each hour until noon. We then greeted Brother Modestino, a dear friend from Pietrelcina. He took us upstairs to visit Padre Pio's room and invited us to go inside. We saw everything that was once used by Padre Pio and we were allowed to touch his many articles. I became very emotional and smelled the strong scent of roses mixed with violets.

Blessed Padre Pio is a special saint. Although the canonization process for him has not yet been completed, I use the term here in the oldest tradition of "saint-making", as the voice of the people, closest to and blessed by, the candidate.

He often repeated the words, "I am a mystery to myself." For fifty years he bore on his body the stigmata, the open wounds that bled—that no doctor nor medicine could heal. From his person emanated the different scents that people could smell for miles away. He had the gift of bilocation, the ability to read hearts and souls and worked countless miracles.

When people thanked him for a miracle they received, he would respond, "Don't thank me, but thank our Lord Jesus Christ."

My Son Enters the Capuchins

In 1973 our son, Pio Francesco, decided to enter the Capuchin Franciscan Seminary in Newton, New Jersey. He wanted to become a Capuchin priest. We were surprised and happy at his vocation, but we advised him to complete high school first. He was 16 years old and doing well in school and soccer. Yet, his desire was very strong.

We accompanied him to the seminary in the fall of 1973. It was a high school seminary for young men interested in the religious life and it was run by the Capuchins. I was sad because I wanted him home for a while longer, but I prayed to Padre Pio to accompany him. The Lord, indeed, gave me a great grace, to be the mother of a priest, especially a Capuchin. Capuchin Franciscans are a reform order of Franciscans adhering closely to the original rule of St. Francis of Assisi.

I have always loved the Capuchins. Padre Pio was a Capuchin Franciscan and I grew up around them in Pietrelcina. Often their friars came to our home to visit with my parents.

On the 6th of July in 1983, the birthday of my son Pio Francesco, I dreamed of Padre Pio. He inquired, "How is Pio Francesco?" I quickly told him that he was still a novice, but after he completed his studies he would be ordained. Padre Pio told me, "You are mistaken. He is not a novice, but is studying Theology. He has made me happy by becoming a priest."

When I awoke, I realized the mistake I had made. Pio was indeed studying Theology and not in the novitiate. Padre Pio corrected me even in my dreams.

Padre Pio's Assistance with
My Son Vincent

In the early months of 1982, my son, Vincent, applied to a medical school in Philadelphia. Although he did very well in his studies, there was considerable competition and a complex selection process was in effect.

On the evening of April 23, 1982, I dreamed of Padre Pio. This was the evening before my son expected the results from his application. Padre Pio embraced me with a smile and then blessed me. The next morning, I interpreted this to be a good sign for Vincent. When he phoned me, I quickly told him that he would have good news from the school. Vincent inquired how I knew. I then told him about my dream. I had asked for the Padre's intercession and the Padre had prayed for him. When Vincent returned to his apartment, that very day, he found the letter of acceptance in his mailbox.

The Padre is near all his children in their joys of life, as the previous stories have shown, but he is even closer to them in their sufferings.

Preparation for Suffering

On September 23, 1983, the fifteenth anniversary of his death, Padre Pio came to me in a dream. He told me, "You have to prepare yourself for a suffering." The following morning, I became preoccupied with the possible meaning of this dream.

The next day I broke out in hives all over my body. The pain was terrible, and the hives itched incessantly. Neither doctors nor medicine helped me. Then on the Feast Day of St. Martin of Tours, November 11th, my problem completely disappeared. This is how it was meant to be: purification through suffering. Padre Pio had come to warn me before it all started.

When my youngest son, Paolo Paris, was in college, I went through a difficult time. My husband was at work, and I too desired to find employment. I dreamed of Padre Pio and drew close to him, confiding my intentions. He replied, "Stay at home. If not, who will cook?" When I told my husband of the dream, he was very pleased. He laughed because he did not know how to cook.

In 1978 when my son Pio was in seminary college, the Padre came to me in a dream and told me: "Prepare to cook many pasta dishes. Now many friars will be coming to your home."

This indeed happened. Throughout the years, I have been in the kitchen a great deal of the time preparing pasta dishes for the friars who have come to visit us. The dream of Padre Pio had a touch of prophecy to it.

My Son's First Mass in Pietrelcina

Shortly before my son, Pio Francesco, was ordained a Capuchin priest, in May 1985, the Padre again came to me in a dream. This time he came with other Capuchins. He said, "I am very happy that your son will be ordained. Come to Italy with your husband and Pio so he can celebrate a first Mass in Pietrelcina and in San Giovanni Rotondo." I told my husband what Padre Pio said and later told my son. We decided to accept our beloved Padre's "invitation".

Pio Francesco Mandato was ordained on June 8, 1985, in Hoboken, New Jersey at St. Ann's Church. Bishop Lawrence Graziano O.F.M., officiated at the ordination. At the end of July, Andre and I accompanied our son to Italy.

The Capuchin friars prepared a beautiful Mass in the church of Our Lady of the Angels. Padre Mario Mancanelli was the pastor, and Padre Gianrico Tanno was the superior. The friars were happy that Pio was celebrating his first Mass in Pietrelcina on August 3, 1985. There was a festive procession with many children in native costumes, along with brothers, priests and seminarians.

Relatives and townspeople participated. The procession began at my parents' home which is in the center of town and made its way to the Church. It was there that the townspeople would wait for the celebration of the first Mass of the newly ordained.

The mass was celebrated at the altar of the *Madonna della Libera*, where Padre Pio had celebrated his first Mass on August 14th, 1910.

We were all moved by the poignant ceremony. Both my husband and I wept with joy and thanked Our Lord for such a wonderful gift - a priest for a son!

Two days later we went to San Giovanni Rotondo. It was here where Pio celebrated Mass in the little chapel where Padre Pio celebrated it for so many years. The friars received us with great hospitality. We prayed at the Padre's tomb, thanking him for his paternal affection and for enlightening me through dreams.

My Father's Death

On October 15, 1985, my brother called me from Italy telling me that my father had died. I became filled with tremendous sorrow. He had been hospitalized for about a week and we had just been together in Italy during August, when my father saw his grandson celebrate his first Mass.

I shed many tears of profound sorrow, but Padre Pio came to me in a dream that night. He drew near, as he sat down in my home and said, "Graziella, don't cry. I know you are sad about your father, but you have to realize that he had (reached) a good age." He embraced me and I woke up. I was greatly consoled by the Padre and thanked him for his comfort and paternal affection.

What Padre Pio pointed out, regarding my father's advanced age, was true. He was 90 years old, and the time had arrived for him to go forth into God's Kingdom and be near the Padre who loved him so much.

On October 14, 1985, the day before my father's death, my brothers were with him in the hospital. My father told them, "Please, thank the beautiful woman who stands by me and holds my hand throughout the day and night." My brothers exchanged glances and said, "Papa must not be in his right mind." My father overheard them and said, "My mind is clear. You must believe me."

My brothers saw nobody present who matched the description of the beautiful woman he described. However, they realized that possibly he was describing Our Blessed Mother who had come to assist him. Both of my parents were very devout, and my father faithfully recited the rosary every day of his entire life.

The 100th Anniversary of Padre Pio's Birth

The centennial of Padre Pio's birth took place on May 25, 1987 in Pietrelcina. My husband, our son Pio and I went together to participate in the festivities. Many came to Pietrelcina from all parts of the world. Hierarchy, clergy, pilgrims, townsfolk - all gathered to celebrate the gift of Padre Pio.

A solemn Mass was held outdoors in the soccer stadium. Preceding the Mass there was a long procession in which the lovely statue of *La Madonna della Libera* was carried. Over one hundred roses were on the altar and imbued the air with a lovely fragrance. At one point, two local planes flew over the stadium, dropping leaflets printed with: "Congratulations, Padre Pio. We love you." It seemed as if they fluttered down from the hands of angels. It was a very moving day, and we all thanked the Lord for giving Padre Pio to Pietrelcina.

The statue of *La Madonna della Libera* was also solemnly venerated and her face seemed to express joy and tenderness. Padre Pio always addressed her as the *Tender Mother* and he would often say, "Tell everyone that I grew up at her feet."

The Feast Day of *La Madonna Della Libera* is celebrated every year in Pietrelcina on the first Sunday in August. All those who emigrated from Pietrelcina return home to celebrate. We too return each August to celebrate, as well as to visit my mother.

Today, thousands go to Pietrelcina to visit the home of Padre Pio, to see where he was born and raised. They visit St. Anne's Church where he was baptized. They go to the place where he meditated and prayed in Piana Romana and where he received the stigmata in 1910.

What a great joy it is for all his spiritual children to know that he is now beatified. Upon the formal recognition of sanctity, he will be referred to as Saint Pio. Churches may then be dedicated to his name and heavenly protection. It is especially joyous for those of us who knew him in Pietrelcina, where he was born, and in San Giovanni Rotondo, where his mortal remains rest.

In the Capuchin friary in Pietrelcina, there is a museum dedicated to Padre Pio. It was set up after his death and many precious relics are on display. A shirt containing the blood from his experience of flagellation is on display, along with the handkerchiefs he used to staunch the blood from his hands and feet. The scourging of Christ, prior to his Crucifixion, is referred to as *The Flagellation*, where His back and shoulders were an open wound of exposed and bleeding flesh. Padre Pio suffered all the wounds of Christ, including the Crown of Thorns, visible only to a select few. A naïve visitor once inquired if the wounds were painful. The Padre responded in Pietrelcinese humor, "Do you think God gave these to me for decoration?"

Also on display are liturgical vestments, his Franciscan Capuchin habit and other objects that Blessed Padre Pio used. I went often to visit the museum and contemplate the significance of all these relics.

My Grandchildren and Padre Pio

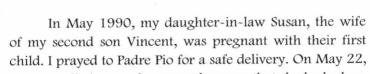

In May 1990, my daughter-in-law Susan, the wife of my second son Vincent, was pregnant with their first child. I prayed to Padre Pio for a safe delivery. On May 22, my son called me and gave us the news that she had a boy. They named him Pio Francis, Padre Pio's very name. We were surprised that they selected that name and I knew how happy the Padre became when children were named after him.

In 1994, when Pio Francis was four years old, I dreamed of Padre Pio. I was attending a Mass, celebrated by my son Pio and my mother, husband and grandson were with me. Padre Pio came near us and asked, "What is your grandson's name? I told him, "He is Pio Francis. They gave him your name." He replied, "Good, good," and placed his hands on the little boy. Every night my Pio Francis and his younger brother Andrew pray to Our Lord and Our Lady. Then they ask for Padre Pio to help them.

The Padre also drew near when my son Paolo Paris and his wife had their children. In April 1996, my daughter-in-law Sheila, was in the hospital experiencing some difficulties with her pregnancy. We decided to ask the Padre to intercede.

On the night of April 29, 1996, Padre Pio came to me in a dream. He was smiling and I interpreted this as a good sign and a blessing. At 7 a.m. the next morning, Paolo Paris called to tell me he had just become a father. They had a little girl and named her Grace, after me. I was deeply touched by their gesture and appreciative that all went well.

Padre Pio also advised me when Paolo had his second child. In August 1997, I was in Italy with my husband. We were attending Mass in Pietrelcina when, after Communion, I smelled a strong scent of perfume. It came twice. I knew it was Padre Pio's odor of sanctity, and I knew a blessing had been given. After Mass, when I went to my mother's house, Paolo Paris called and told us that Sheila had just given birth to a son, whom they named Pietro Paris. I then asked Paolo if he remembered that Padre Pio wanted me to name him Pietro. Paolo responded, "Mamma, Sheila is the one who chose the name Pietro, and she had no idea that Padre Pio had wanted me to be called Pietro. I couldn't believe it! I felt that Padre Pio confirmed his intercession by the scent of his perfume at Mass.

Padre Pio's Presence in Dreams

As all my accounts have shown, I have felt Padre Pio's presence throughout my entire life. Many times he has come to me in dreams. Other times I have been blessed by his fragrance of sanctity.

When Padre Pio was alive, I was fortunate enough to visit him in person. However after his death, he has spoken to me in dreams. Whenever I have invoked his protection, I have felt him near, especially in moments of need.

I am grateful to have kept a record of all my visits with the Padre, going back to the first time I met him, and even more grateful to be able to witness to these facts. On May 31, 1992, Padre Pio came to me in a dream. Along with my husband and mother, I found myself in the church in Pietrelcina. On the left side of the church I saw Padre Pio lying on a bed in great pain. Next to him was Our Lady of Sorrows, dressed all in black. They were speaking to each other and looking at me. Both were very sad. When Our Lady left, I saw that Padre Pio's stigmatized feet were bleeding profusely. My son Pio was next to Padre Pio.

The following morning I was preoccupied about the significance of this dream. My husband simply said that Padre Pio's bleeding stigmata was a sign of grace. Later that morning I decided to go shopping, and as I entered the store I noticed that the front section was wet, I slid and in an instant, fell to the ground. As much as I tried, I failed to get up and remained on the ground, immobilized. An ambulance came and brought me to the hospital, where they discovered a small fracture. I had to have physical therapy and after some time, I began to improve.

The Padre and Our Lady showed me through the dream that I was about to undergo a terrible moment, but they were also there to help me. Padre Pio's bleeding feet were a sign of grace, as my husband had said. Although I had to experience this mishap, I believe I was protected from something much worse.

In May 1993, the doctors discovered that my husband had prostrate problems and would require surgery. We were both very distressed. Our son, Vincent, knew of specialists in Philadelphia and we decided to go there for the surgery. I again turned to Padre Pio, asking him to intercede.

On June 20, he appeared in my dream and simply looked at me with a smile. The next day, June 21, when my husband had his surgery, all truly went well. My husband said afterwards, with tears in his eyes, "Padre Pio was near." Together we thanked Padre Pio for his intercessions with Our Lord.

In March 1998, I was not well and began to suffer much. I prayed and asked for relief. After falling asleep, I dreamed of Padre Pio, who was sitting on a chair in Pietrelcina. I saw him and went to him. He said, "I can't do anything for you." However, he allowed me to kiss his hand.

The whole day I tried to understand the meaning of his words. I cried, "Oh, Holy Padre, what must I do? Is this suffering allowed by the Lord? If it is, I must accept this suffering and do God's will.

For comfort, I called to mind some of the Padre's sayings. One of his was: "Suffering is a gift from God. Blessed is he who is able to profit by it."

Another one was: "Pray, hope and don't agitate your spirit. Anxiety doesn't lead to anything. God is merciful and will hear your prayer."

CONCLUSION

Thanks be to God and to Padre Pio that I have been able to complete this writing. I will never tire of thanking God for the great gift he has given to the world in our times......a friar who has become for all, a protective father.

My dear spiritual father Sunday, June 16, 2002, you will be canonized by our Holy Father, Pope John Paul II. May Our Lord be praised.

Thank you, dear spiritual Father. You have loved me while you were on this earth and you have loved me even more, now that you are in heaven.

In union with my whole family, we place ourselves under your protection.

DEVOTIONALS

The following ninety selections are suitable for use as daily devotionals. They have been taken from the writings of Padre Pio of Pietrelcina, Letters I & II

Day 1

As soon as we are aware of becoming discouraged we must revive our faith and abandon ourselves to the arms of the Divine Father who is always ready to receive us, always that is, if we go to Him sincerely.

Day 2

I know that a soul in which God dwells always fears to offend God at every step and this fear becomes almost insupportable, if this holy fear overflows into the execution of our very duties. But a soul in such a state should be consoled because it is precisely because of this fear that it will not stumble but make progress.

Day 3

Oh the lovely month of May. It is the most beautiful month of the year. Yes, dear Father how well this month preaches the tenderness and beauty of Mary!

When I think of the innumerable benefits received from this dear Mother, I am ashamed of myself, for I have never sufficiently appreciated her heart and her hand which have bestowed these benefits upon me with so much love, and what troubles me most is that I have repaid the affectionate care of this Mother of ours by continually offending her.

How often have I confided to this Mother the painful anxieties that trouble my heart! And how often has she consoled me!

~

Love the Blessed Mother and make the Blessed Mother loved.

Day 4

May Jesus be always in your mind, in your heart, and before your eyes. May He invariably be your beginning, your continuation and your end and absorb your entire life into Himself. May Jesus' Mother and ours obtain for us from her Son the grace to live entirely for the heart of God, a completely interior life although hidden in Him.

Day 5

Jesus will never abandon you! I ask you to pray hard for the efficacy of my ministry. I am afraid of displeasing the Lord in the exercise of my priestly activity. May Jesus arrange all things for His glory and our salvation.

Day 6

All things can serve the Master of our souls who works only for good. Those souls most afflicted are the favorites of the divine heart.

Voice of Padre Pio Volume XXIV

Day 7

The sensual passions are the most enticing and they find an outlet in a great many different acts, which the Apostle enumerates: fornication, impurity, licentiousness, lust and avarice. (Gal 5:9) The last named gains such mastery over the soul infected by it that it becomes the idol of that soul to which it sacrifices everything else.

Day 8

I strive only to obey you, the good God, having made known to me the one for me to hope for salvation and to sing of victory.

Day 9

I know that before Jesus and in the most sacred Heart of Jesus your heart beats with a holy affection for your neighbors too. I know how you ardently desire the salvation of souls; at this I am certain and pleased at the wonderful action of divine grace in you. However, the cause of all this is our Lord's goodness and the total renunciation of your will, made through my hands out of love for you.

Day 10

I repeat to you ~ remember the palm of victory reserved for those who suffer in order to be perfected. The more the darkness increases, the closer God is.

Day 11

The most beautiful credo is that which comes from our lips in darkness, in sacrifice and suffering, in a supreme act of an infallible will towards goodness; like a flash of lightning it rents asunder the darkness in our soul, and in the midst of the storm raises one to God.

Day 12

The devil is roaring and shouting continuously around my poor will. All I can do is say with firm resolution, although without any feeling:

"Praise be to Jesus... I believe."

Day 13

I confess in the first place that for me it is a great misfortune to be unable to express and pour out this ever-active volcano which burns me up and which Jesus has placed in this very small heart. It can all be summed up as follows: I am consumed by love for God and love for my neighbor.

Day 14

May Jesus enable you to appreciate more and more, along with all the souls who love Him, with a sincere and pure heart His most loving invitation "My yoke is easy and my burden is light!"

Day 15

Oh open your heart to this Father the most loving of all fathers and let Him act freely within you. Let us not be stingy with one who enables us even too much, whose generosity is endless and knows no limits.

Day 16

Let your only thought be to love God and to grow more in virtue and in holy love which is the bond of Christian perfection.

Day 17

In all life's events recognize the divine will, adore and bless it. Especially in the things that are hardest for you, do not be in a hurry to escape from them. Raise up your heart to the Divine Father more than ever on these occasions.

Day 18

As long as you fear to offend Him, you already love Him and no longer offend Him.

Day 19

The virtue of love is exceedingly beautiful, and to enkindle it in our hearts the Son of God was pleased to come down Himself from the bosom of the eternal Father, to become like us in order to teach us and make it easy for us, with the means He left us, to acquire this most eminent virtue.

Day 20

Grow always in Christian love and never tire of advancing in this which is the queen of all virtues. Consider that you can never grow too much in this most beautiful virtue. Love it very much. Let it be more than the apple of your eye, for it is truly most dear to our Divine Master.

Day 21

Live in such a way that you may be able to repeat at every moment with the Apostle St. Paul, "Be imitators of me, as I am of Jesus Christ. Live in such a way, I repeat that the world will be forced to say of you, here is Christ."

Day 22

I give infinite thanks for you to the Lord who is so good to all His creatures, especially to those who do their utmost to love Him. He never ceases to visit them in time of truth and to send down a heavenly charism into their souls, which most serve them as armor and shield to ward off the blows of the enemy and further misfortunes. Praise be for ever to Jesus and may the divine mercy and providence be praised forever.

Day 23

When you are overcome with sadness at sunset, then more than ever must you renew your trust in God, humble yourself before Him and praise and bless the heavenly Father with a full heart.

Day 24

A soul who trusts in her Lord and places all her hope in Him has nothing to fear. The enemy of our salvation is always around us to snatch from our hearts the anchor that is to lead us to salvation, by which I mean trust in God our Father.

Day 25

Let us keep a very firm hold on this anchor and not relinquish it for a single moment. Otherwise all would be lost. Repeat continually and more especially in the darkest hours those most beautiful words of Job: Even if you are to slay me, oh, Lord, I will hope in you!

Day 26

Always be on guard and don't become puffed up, considering yourself to be good in any way, or above others. Don't imagine that you are better than them or at least as good, but consider all to be better than yourself.

Day 27

Let us bless the Lord for He is good, for His mercy endures forever! May Jesus lighten your load of sorrow and enable you to walk invariably along the path that leads to Him.

Day 28

Thus we shall end our life in the holy kiss of the Lord, an admirable kiss of divine condescension by which, according to St. Bernard (sermons in Cantica) is not a matter of approaching face-to-face and mouth-to-mouth. Rather does it mean that the creator draws close to His creature and man and God are united for all eternity.

Day 29

Oh my God and my glory then alone can we say Yes, oh Divine Lover, O Lord of our life, Your love is better than wine, Your anointing oils are fragrant.

Day 30

Let us be glad for one day we shall sing more joyful hymns to our most tender lover Who is the sweetest repose of our hearts, enamored of His beauty. Let us rejoice, I say, for the day will come, as I hope, on which our hearts will no longer be torn by cruel remorse for not loving our sweet Lord sufficiently.

Day 31

Through Jacob man vanquished an angel and in Jesus Christ the whole of mankind vanquished God: "You have striven with God and men and have prevailed." (Genesis 32:28)

What was the secret of such an immense triumph by which the patriarch Jacob overcame an angel? One of the prophets has told us: humility, tears and prayer.

Day 32

In the meantime let us prepare ourselves for this great day and if we love Jesus let us now stir ourselves up and keep far from all that smacks of worldliness. Let us reflect well that all the sufferings of this world, according to St. Paul are not worth comparing with the glory that awaits us.

Day 33

Every minister of the Lord ought to work continually for the good of souls. He ought never admit weariness and never say, "I have worked too hard for the souls of others." This is the image of a genuine catholic priest.

Day 34

Always place your confidence in Jesus and He will know how to comfort your soul even when it is tossed about in a stormy sea. Never be afraid of the enemy's enticements, for no matter how strong they may be they will never avail to sweep you into his nets as long as you remain faithful to the Lord and on your guard, while you build up your strength by prayer and holy humility.

Day 35

God has promised that He opposes the proud but gives grace to the humble; that these who watch and pray will not enter into temptation. (James 4:6; 1 Peter 5:5)

Day 36

It is true that God's power triumphs over everything, but humble and suffering prayer prevails over God Himself. It stops His hand, extinguishes His lightning, disarms Him, vanquishes and placates Him, and makes Him almost a dependent and a friend.

Day 37

Let us approach to receive the bread of angels with great faith and with a great flame of love in our hearts: Let us await this most tender lover of our souls in order to be consoled in this life with the kiss of His mouth.   Happy are we, Raffaelina, if we succeed in receiving the consolation of this kiss in the present life!   Then indeed will we feel our will inseparably bound at all times to Jesus' will and nothing in the world can prevent us from willing what our Divine Master wills.

Day 38

The enemies are continually rising up, Father, against the ship of my spirit and they cry out in unison: "Let us knock him down, let us crush him, since he is weak and cannot hold out much longer." Alas, my dear Father, who will set me free from these roaring lions all ready to devour me? You say only too well that while the Lord is testing us by His crosses and sufferings, He always leaves in our hearts a glimmer of light by which we continue to have great trust in Him and to see His immense goodness.

This light, in fact, has never grown less, but you will have to agree that it is precisely this light which causes the soul greater pain than can be humanly conceived. It shows up the divine goodness as something the soul cannot enjoy by loving possession, something it can only long for from afar with painful yearnings to possess it. This light makes the soul yearn for God, the source of all good , and more often than not the pain of its desire is revealed by abundant tears.

Day 39

St. Paul has also disclosed to us the secret of the strength, by which Jesus Christ, who took on Himself our miserable human flesh, vanquished God in all His glory, that is by humbling himself by prayer; weeping and loud cries: "With loud cries and tears and He was heard for His Godly fear." (Hebrews 5:7)

Day 40

Turning to the state of the Christian in times of adversity, the holy Apostles want them to show patience and to stifle all resentment either internal or external. He expects him to bear with all the vexatious behavior of others and to forgive them sincerely.

Day 41

In the battles of life, he who trembles before this same God against whose strength nothing is of any avail, for everything yields to His word, everything vanishes at the mere sight of His word.

He, I say, who is bowed beneath the weight of tribulation, who is crushed by the sight of the wounds produced by his own failings and drags himself along face downward in the dust, who humbles himself, weeps, sighs and prays. This man triumphs over God's justice and obliges God to show him mercy: "She besought Him with tears and was powerful." (Esther 8:3 Genesis 32:28)

~

Place your hearts in the state of complete confidence in God.

Day 42

For pity's sake, let us flee from these useless fears the moment they rise up in us. Let us never despair of the divine assistance. Would this not be an offense against the divine mercy? When these fears well up within you remember the true Jacob who prayed in the garden. Remember that he discovered there the true ladder that connects earth with heaven; (Gen 28:12) He showed us that humility, contrition and prayer abolish the distance between man and God.

Day 43

"Tell everyone that I grew up at her feet"

Padre Pio about the Madonna della Libera

Day 44

May the motives of faith and the comfort of Christian hope offer you continual support in all of this. If you act in this way the heavenly Father will alleviate your trial with the balm of His goodness and mercy. The holy and beneficent angel of faith, moreover, counsels and urges us to have recourse to insistent humble prayer to the goodness and mercy of the heavenly Father in the firm hope that we will be heard.

Day 45

May Jesus continue with His Divine chrism, may He increase more and more your thirst for His heavenly love to the point of complete satiation. May He enable it to be shared by all those whose names, through His divine mercy and their own response, are written in the book of eternal life. Amen.

Day 46

May your heart always be the temple of the Holy Spirit and may Jesus come to you in your present distress and trial. May He always be the helmsman of your little spiritual ship. May Mary be the star which shines on your path and may she show you the way to reach the heavenly Father. May she be like an anchor to which you must be more closely attached in time of trial.

Day 47

The fact of feeling in no way attracted to any place whatsoever in this ignoble world cannot have its origin in anyone but God, who wants in this way to detach the soul from everything but Himself.

Day 48

Offer, moreover, to the glory of His divine Majesty the rest you are about to take and never forget your guardian angel who is close to you, who never leaves you no matter how badly you treat him. Oh unspeakable excellence of this good angel for us! How many times have I made him weep when I refused to comply with his wishes, which were also God's wishes!

May this most faithful friend of ours save us from further unfaithfulness. Try to have in mind some thought concerning the Passion of Jesus before you fall asleep. I advise you as you go to sleep to have before your mental gaze the picture of Jesus as He prayed in the garden.

Day 49

I therefore urge you in the charity of Christ to make sure you calm your anxiety by drinking at the fountain of divine love, which you must do by faith and trust, by humility and submission to God's will. The Venerable St. Therese of the Child Jesus: "I am a little soul I choose neither to live nor to die but may Jesus do as He pleases with me."

Day 50

Let us not cease then, to kiss the Divine Son in this way, for if these are the kisses we give Him now, He Himself will come as He has promised, full of mercy and love.

Day 51

My daughter I beg you not to become weary of asking the divine Bridegroom, the spouse of the sacred song, for this kiss of peace, which is a truly delightful paradise. By this kiss you will defy all the vain fears of this world, the devil's prompting, the enticements of the flesh and without losing an iota of your calm you will overcome all these things and win a full victory over them.

Day 52

Do not refrain from asking Jesus for this blessed kiss through a feeling of false humility, which would be in reality a most refined form of pride by the wise one of this world.

Day 53

Do you mean to say you don't know that anyone who refuses human remedies exposes himself to the danger of offending the Lord? And do you not know that God tells us through the sacred scriptures to love the physician for love of Himself? (Sirach 38:1)

Day 54

Don't ever fall back on yourself when the storm is raging. Place all your trust in the heart of our most sweet Jesus who is not only mine but your Jesus also. Renew your faith continually and never give it up, for faith never abandons' anyone, much less a soul that is yearning to love God.

Day 55

Pray constantly and you will thus win the victory over our enemies. Humble yourself beneath the powerful hand of the heavenly physician and thus, when heavenly nuptials are celebrated Jesus will have you sit in the first place at the banquet table, for God has promised that whoever humbles himself will be exalted. (Matt 23)

Day 56

To be worried because something we have done has not turned out in accordance with our pure intention shows a lack of humility. This is a clear sign that the person concerned has not entrusted the success of his action to the divine assistance but has depended too much on his own strength.

Day 57

Never let your mind become so absorbed in your work or other matters as to make you lose the presence of God.

Day 58

To put it briefly, let us make an effort to ensure that the supper by which we satisfy the body may be a preparation for the altogether divine supper of the most Holy Eucharist.

Day 59

Oh, how sublime is the beautiful virtue of charity, which the Son of God has brought us! All must have it at heart, but more so still those who aim at holiness

Day 60

Anger is a moral passion, which also exists in good people and in itself is not sinful. But if we do not know how to control it, it becomes sinful, as happens when we are angry with someone who does not deserve it, or before we have reason to be angry, or in matters which do not justify our anger.

Day 61

Unfortunately, we are never done trying to improve our appearance. Indeed all our efforts are directed towards improving the body and making it more beautiful. Less attention is perhaps devoted to the soul, which we may have treated as a negligible quantity.

Day 62

The soul's cooperation with divine grace is all that is required to enable it to develop, to reach such a degree of splendor and beauty as to attract, not so much the loving and astonished gaze of the angels, but the gaze of God Himself according to the testimony of Holy Scripture: "The King, that is God, will desire your beauty." (Ps 45:11)

Day 63

The other life is a supernatural one received from Jesus at baptism and therefore a spiritual, heavenly life by which we practice virtue. Baptism brings about a real transformation in us. We die to sin and are grafted onto Jesus Christ in such a way as to live by His very life.

Day 64

May God be blessed forever, for He alone knows how to bring about these marvels in a soul that always resisted Him, a soul that was the receptacle of an infinite amount of filth. He willed to make me an example of grace and He is pleased to hold me up to sinners as a model so that none may despair. Let sinners then, fix their gaze on me, the greatest sinner of all, and let them hope in God.

Day 65

Now if baptism causes every Christian to die to the first life and rise up to the second, it is the duty of each Christian to seek the things of heaven and not to care about the things of this earth.

Day 66

The Christian Vocation, I say, requires that we do not attach our hearts to this miserable world. The good Christian who really follows his vocation directs all his attention, all his study to securing eternal possession.

Day 67

He must look on the things of this world below in such a way as to esteem and appreciate only those which help him to obtain eternal things and must despise all things which do not help him to attain what is eternal.

Day 68

The Christian who has forgotten his true vocation and is merely a Christian in name, a worldly Christian, judges things quite differently. His judgment is the exact opposite to that of the Christian worthy of the name who lives according to the spirit of Jesus Christ. The former judges things from the point of view of their capacity to satisfy his vanity and his passions. The latter, on the other hand, judges them in relation to eternal things.

Day 69

St. James tells us: Let every man be slow to anger for the anger of man does not work the righteousness of God. (James 1:19-20).

Day 70

The Christian then, who has died and risen again with the Christ by baptism, must invariably strive to renew and improve himself by contemplating the eternal truths and the will of God. In a word, he must endeavor all the time to reproduce in himself the image of the Lord who created him.

Day 71

Resentment is an offshoot of anger. It is present when a person considers others unworthy to possess what they have and would like to see them humiliated and disgraced by punishment.

Day 72

See then, my dear sister how great a dignity is ours. However, we are great on condition that we preserve sanctifying grace and, alas, how wretched we become when we lose that grace.

Day 73

Turning to the state of the Christian in times of adversity, the holy Apostles want them to show patience and to stifle all resentment either internal or external. He expects them to bear with all the vexatious behavior of others and to forgive them sincerely.

Day 74

May your heart invariably be the temple of the Holy Spirit. May Jesus be the specific King of your soul, to console and bless you and make you holy. Amen.

Day 75

Father, may I be allowed to express myself freely at least to you: I am crucified by love! I can no longer go on. This is too delicate a food for one accustomed to coarse fare and it is for this reason that it continually causes me extreme spiritual indigestion to the point at which my poor soul cried out in acute pain and love at the same time.

Day 76

My wretched soul cannot adapt to this new manner of the Lord's dealings with it. Thus the kiss and the touch, which I would describe as substantial that this most loving heavenly Father imprints on my soul, still causes me extreme suffering.

Day 77

May the grace of the divine Spirit be more and more superabundant in your heart and may most holy Mary watch by your side, so that the divine action within you may obtain even more fully all the fruits the Lord desires.

Day 78

My soul is full of gratitude to God for the many victories it obtains at every instant, and I cannot refrain from uttering endless hymns of blessing to this great and magnificent God. Blessed be the Lord for His great mercy! Eternal praise be to such tender and loving compassion.

Day 79

Dear Father the great glory the divine Lover reserves in heaven for those souls who continue steadfastly to do His will at all times until death, fills my soul with extreme remorse and pierces my heart with sharpest pain. Can it ever be possible for a soul to forget the great dignity due to it's noble destiny and have the temerity to lift it's head proudly against such a Lover?

Day 80

In the midst of this torment I find strength to utter a painful fiat! Oh how sweet and yet how bitter is this "May thy will be done!." It cuts and heals wounds and cures, it deals death and at the same time gives life! Oh sweet torments why are you so unbearable and so lovable simultaneously.

Day 81

Dear God! I come to you in deep confusion, to you who are what you are, while I myself am a miserable nonentity worthy of your contempt and commiseration. But I realize that I am dealing with God and that He is mine. Ah, yes, who can deny that He is mine.

Day 82

Dear Father, I cannot survive this pain, which threatens to annihilate me. I feel my life slipping away and at this moment I cannot tell you whether I am alive or not. I am beside myself. Pain and tenderness combine to reduce my soul to a state of bittersweet infirmity.

Day 83

The embraces of my Beloved, which follow one another in great profusion, I should say incessantly, immeasurably and unsparingly, cannot extinguish in my soul the acute pain caused by my inadequacy to bear the weight of an infinite love.

Day 84

My Dear Father, may Jesus possess you in heaven. Just as you possess Him sacramentally in your hands every day!

Day 85

I tremble once more as I write to you. But why do I tremble? I find it almost impossible to explain the action of the Beloved. In the immensity of His strength infinite love has at last overcome my hardheartedness, leaving me weak and powerless. He keeps pouring Himself completely into the small vase of this creature and I suffer an unspeakable martyrdom because of my inability to bear the weight of this immense love.

Day 86

How can I carry the infinite in this little heart of mine? How can I continue to confine him to the narrow cell of my soul? My soul is melting with pain and love, with bitterness and tenderness simultaneously.

Day 87

How can I endure such immense suffering inflicted by the Most High? Because of the exaltation of possessing him in me, I cannot refrain from saying with the most holy Virgin: "My spirit rejoices in God my Savior" (Luke 1:47) Possessing Him within me, I am impelled to say with the spouse of the Sacred Song "I found Him whom my soul loves; I held Him and would not let Him go." (Song 3:4)

Day 88

Still, my dear Father, I have a great desire to suffer for the love of Jesus. How is it, then, that when I am put to the test, altogether against my will I seek relief? What force and violence must I use towards myself in these trials to reduce nature to silence when it cries out loud, so to speak, for consolation!

Day 89

May Jesus continue to possess your heart and may His grace accompany and sustain you in all the trials of love to which He may be pleased to subject you!

Day 90

I beg you not to worry about your own soul. Jesus loves you all the time and when Jesus loves, what is there to fear? Be careful all the time not to let your occupations upset your spiritual life and cause you anxiety, and although you set out over the waves and against the wind of many perplexities, keep your gaze fixed upwards and say to Our Lord continually: "Dear God, I am rowing and sailing for You; be my pilot and my oarsman Yourself".

Have no fear of anything! Be consoled, for when you reach the haven, the delights you will enjoy will compensate you for the hardships endured in getting there.

May Jesus always take His repose in your heart and allow you to rest at His feet.

NOVENA ~ ROSARY ~ PRAYERS

Novena to the Sacred Heart of Jesus

O my Jesus, You said, *"Truly I say to you, ask and you shall receive, seek and you shall find, knock and it shall be opened to you"*, behold I knock, I seek and I ask for the grace of...

Our Father, Hail Mary, Glory be to the Father, Sacred Heart of Jesus, I place all my trust in You.

O my Jesus, You said, *"Truly I say to you, if you ask anything of the Father in my name, He will give it to you."* Behold, in Your name, I ask the Father for the grace of...

Our Father, Hail Mary, Glory be to the Father, Sacred Heart of Jesus, I place my trust in You.

O my Jesus, You said: *"Truly I say to you, heaven and earth will pass away, but My words will not pass away."* Behold, encouraged by Your infallible words, I now ask for the grace of...

Our Father, Hail Mary, Glory be to the Father, Sacred Heart of Jesus, I place my trust in You.

O Sacred Heart of Jesus, *For Whom it is impossible not to have compassion on the afflicted, have pity on us miserable sinners and grant us the grace which we ask of You, through the Sorrowful and Immaculate Heart of Mary, Your tender Mother and ours.*

Hail Holy Queen...St. Joseph, foster father of Jesus, pray for us.

This novena prayer was recited every day by Padre Pio for all those who asked for his prayers. The faithful are invited to recite it daily, so as to be spiritually united with the prayer of Padre Pio.

Graziella's Prayer to Padre Pio

Padre Pio intercede for me before Jesus. You who are full of love obtain blessings for my heart.

Jesus, I unite myself to Padre Pio's prayer. For the love you bear for him, bring consolation to my heart.

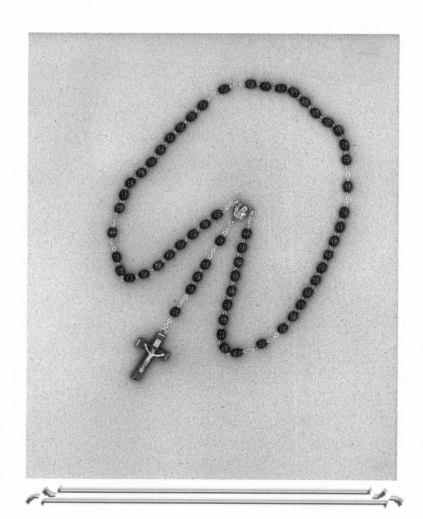

The Healing Rosary of
Our Mother of Perpetual Help

(from the Prayer Companion Booklet OMPH)

SIGN OF THE CROSS

In the name of the Father and the Son and the Holy Spirit. Amen.

THE APOSTLE'S CREED

I believe in God, the Father Almighty, Creator of heaven and earth; and in Jesus Christ, His only Son, Our Lord; Who was conceived by the Holy Spirit, born of the Virgin Mary, suffered under Pontius Pilate, was crucified, died and was buried. He descended into hell; the third day He rose again from the dead; He ascended into heaven, sits at the right hand of God, the Father Almighty; from thence He shall come to judge the living and the dead. I believe in the Holy Spirit, the holy Catholic Church, the communion of saints, the forgiveness of sins, the resurrection of the body, and life everlasting. Amen.

Let us pray for the virtues of Faith, Hope and Love and for the intentions of the Holy Father.

Our Father, 3 Hail Mary's, Glory Be, Fatima Prayer

OUR FATHER

Our Father, Who art in Heaven, hallowed be Thy name; Thy Kingdom come; Thy will be done on earth as it is in heaven. Give us this day our daily bread; and forgive us our trespasses, as we forgive those who trespass against us; and lead us not into temptation, but deliver us from evil. Amen.

HAIL MARY

Hail Mary, full of grace; the Lord is with thee. Blessed art thou among women, and blessed is the fruit of thy womb, Jesus. Holy Mary, Mother of God, pray for us sinners, now and at the hour of our death. Amen.

GLORY BE TO THE FATHER

Glory be to the Father, and to the Son, and to the Holy Spirit. As it was in the beginning, is now, and ever shall be, world without end. Amen.

FATIMA PRAYER

Oh my Jesus, forgive us our sins and save us from the fires of hell. Lead all the souls to heaven, especially those in most need of Thy mercy.

CONCLUDING PRAYERS OF
THE MOST HOLY ROSARY

To be recited at the end of the Rosary

HAIL HOLY QUEEN

Hail Holy Queen, Mother of Mercy, our life, our sweetness and our hope. To you do we cry, poor banished children of Eve. To you do we send our sighs, mourning and weeping in this valley of tears. Turn then, O most gracious advocate, your eyes of mercy towards us; and after this our exile show unto us the blessed fruit of your womb, Jesus. O clement, O loving, O sweet Virgin Mary. Pray for us, O Holy Mother of God that we may be worthy of the promises of Christ.

Let us pray...

O God, whose only-begotten Son, by his life, death and resurrection has purchased for us the rewards of eternal life; grant we beseech you, that, while meditating on these mysteries of the most holy Rosary of the Blessed Virgin Mary, we may imitate what they contain, and obtain what they promise, through the same Christ Our Lord. Amen.

PRAYER TO ST. MICHAEL

SAINT MICHAEL the Archangel, defend us in battle; be our protection against the wickedness and snares of the devil; may God rebuke him, we humbly pray; and do thou, O Prince of the heavenly host, by the power of God, thrust into hell Satan and all evil spirits who wander through the work, seeking the ruin of souls. Amen.

THE MEMORARE

Remember, O most gracious Virgin Mary, that never was it known that anyone who fled to your protection implored your help or sought your intercession, was left unaided. Inspired by this confidence, I fly unto you, O Virgin of virgins, my Mother. To you do I come; before you I stand, sinful and sorrowful. O Mother of the Word Incarnate, despise not my petitions, but in your mercy hear and answer me. Amen.

A.M.  **D.G.**

THE JOYFUL MYSTERIES

1. The Annunciation
2. The Visitation
3. The Birth of Jesus
4. The Presentation of Jesus in the Temple
5. The Finding of Jesus in the Temple

THE LIVING MYSTERIES

1. Jesus is Tempted in the Desert
2. The Wedding Feast at Cana
3. Jesus Cures the Sick
4. Jesus Feeds the Five Thousand
5. The First Eucharist

THE SORROWFUL MYSTERIES

1. The Agony in the Garden
2. The Scourging at the Pillar
3. The Crowning with Thorns
4. The Carrying of the Cross
5. The Crucifixion and Death of Jesus

THE GLORIOUS MYSTERIES

1. The Resurrection of our Lord
2. The Ascension into Heaven
3. The Descent of the Holy Spirit
4. The Assumption of Mary
5. The Coronation of Mary

Our Lady of Perpetual Help

Look at the picture. Frightened by the vision of two angels showing Him the instruments of the Passion, the Christ Child has to run to His Mother, almost losing, in His haste one of the tiny sandals. Mary holds Him in Her arms reassuringly, lovingly. But notice Her eyes. They look not at Jesus, but at us. Is this not a touch of genius? How better to express Our Lady's plea to us - to avoid sin and love Her Son?

Christ's little Hands, too, are pressed into Mary's as a reminder to us that, just as on earth He placed Himself entirely in Her hands for protection, so now in Heaven He places each of us into her tender loving care.

THE HEALING ROSARY OF OUR MOTHER OF PERPETUAL HELP

The Healing Rosary of Our Mother of Perpetual Help is a new audio production from Angelus Media Distribution Group, combining the recitation of the Holy Rosary with prayerful meditations and original and popular sacred music compositions.

It contains recitations of *The Joyful Mysteries, The Sorrowful Mysteries* and *The Glorious Mysteries,* with special prayer meditations, as well as *The Living Mysteries,* developed through the encouragement of Pope John Paul II, to provide additional opportunities for the faithful to contemplate the saving actions of

Jesus, as portrayed in the Gospel accounts. It carries the Imprimatur of Anthony Cardinal Bevilaqua, D.D., J.C.D., J.D., Archbishop of Philadelphia. The English version has prayers led by Father George Keaveny, C.Ss.R. and the Healing Meditations are led by Father Michael Barrett, C.Ss.R. The Spanish version features Tony Melendez singing beautiful original songs of devotion.

The *Healing Rosary of Our Mother of Perpetual Help* is available in both English and Spanish on double audio cassettes or double compact discs..

A.M.  **D.G.**

We hope you have enjoyed reading *Padre Pio, Encounters with a Spiritual Daughter from Pietrelcina* by Graziella DeNunzio Mandato.

If you would like additional copies of the book and/or copies of *The Healing Rosary of Our Mother of Perpetual Help,* please ask for them at your local Catholic bookstore or call *A.M.D.G.'*s toll free order line 888.222.2634.